ADHD And The Criminal Justice System

To order additional copies, please contact us.
BookSurge, LLC
www.booksurge.com
1-866-308-6235
orders@booksurge.com

PATRICK J. HURLEY, ADHD COACH
AND
ROBERT EME, PH.D.

ADHD AND THE CRIMINAL JUSTICE SYSTEM

SPINNING OUT OF CONTROL

2004

ADHD And The Criminal Justice System

TABLE OF CONTENTS

ABOUT THE COVER

We believe that the cover of the book is a wonderfully apt symbol for ADHD. It is a child's toy top spinning around surrounded by symbols of the criminal justice system.

ADHD is like having a brain that, like a top that is rotating too slowly, is spinning with a wobble. Like a tornado it could be a level one and cause a few complications in a person's life. It can also range up to be similar to a level five tornado that destroys everything and everybody in its path.

Proper treatment can speed up the brain and like a faster spinning top; bring it into balance, therefore transforming a catastrophic tornado of a life into one that is successful.

Special thanks to Gina Pera, who helped us with editing and in so many other ways.

FORWARD

This book is based on the most current scientific literature as well as our own experiences. Since we are a former deputy sheriff and adult probation officer in Iowa and a psychologist from Illinois, the many different operations of the criminal justice system from around the world and even this country could not be adequately researched. Therefore our writing will be about what we know and the criminal justice system as we know it.

Many areas of this country and other countries will no doubt operate differently but we are certain our readers will have the capability to adapt those differences into their particular systems and benefit from the concepts which we present.

We also realize that most police officers deal more with law abiding citizens than they do with traffic violators and the criminal element. Most police tactics and training is designed to deal with worse case scenarios and officer protection and therefore can be viewed by the average citizen as going overboard or antagonistic. Unfortunately in today's day and era, officers for their own protection, and that of society, must operate safely and treat each contact with anyone more cautiously than they would like to.

The book is not meant to answer all questions for all people. It was intentionally written as a short book. It is hoped that it will create an interest in the subject of how ADHD interacts with the criminal justice system. This increased awareness will then lead to increased research, better training, identification, and recognition of ADHD and make the criminal justice system operate more efficiently as well as give those with ADHD a better opportunity to succeed.

We have extensively indexed and cross indexed the book so

that if you are looking for a particular area we hope that you can find it in the back section.

*This book is dedicated to our wives, Candace and Maureen,
for the simple reason that they put up with us.*

*Love,
Pat & Bob*

INTRODUCTION

P icture a child's toy top spinning on a table. When it spins at top speed, it operates efficiently and in balance. As the top slows, it shifts slightly from its perfect balance and begins to wobble. As it slows further, the wobble becomes more pronounced. The toy begins a random dance around the tabletop. Finally, it races out of control, lurching wildly until it careens off the table or falls over.

Many people are born with brains that operate like balanced, high-speed spinning tops. Others go through life with brains that resemble the slowing top, sending these people in random, destructive directions. We know some of them by labels such as "defendant," "probationer," "parolee," or "inmate"—people who end up in our country's criminal justice system with a highly treatable but often overlooked disability: Attention Deficit Hyperactivity Disorder (ADHD). In fact, an astounding 30 to 70 percent of inmates may have ADHD.[1]

This means that, at a minimum, one out of every three persons accused of a crime and appearing before criminal-justice professionals has ADHD. These professionals include judges, prosecutors, defense attorneys, jail staff, and parole-boards members plus probation, corrections, law enforcement, and parole officers. Imagine a justice system that is educated about the traits and often serious consequences of ADHD.

That is the purpose of this book: to provide criminal justice professionals with clear, practical advice and information—based on the best of current science—that will prove useful on a daily basis.

Numerous books discuss ADHD in adults and children, but

no other book exists to help professionals in the criminal justice system better understand and work with people who have ADHD.

In the criminal justice system, everything begins with the police. Few enter the criminal justice system unless the police arrest them. As you will see in Chapter 4, "The Initial Law Enforcement Contact," the police are identifying people with ADHD every day; they just don't realize it. As the person moves through the criminal justice system, still more opportunities exist to identify those who have ADHD. Identifying them can not only improve their lives but also in some cases even save their lives, as shown in the story of David, in Chapter 2. In addition, trained law enforcement officers can use this information to better handle these people in the field in a safer manner. Furthermore, the prosecutors, courts, probation, prisons, and parole professionals can use tax dollars more effectively and potentially reduce recidivism.

Nothing in this book should be construed to suggest that ADHD should or can be an excuse for law-breaking or inappropriate behavior. Each person in life is dealt limitations and challenges. We all have to deal with those in the best way we can. At the same time, this book will explain how ADHD includes undeniable behavioral impairments. Yet it is a treatable disorder. By identifying ADHD individuals earlier and improving their quality of life, society in general will benefit, too, in lowered recidivism, safer communities, and, hopefully, savings to taxpayers.

Lastly, note that though our book focuses on individuals with ADHD in the criminal justice system, the majority of people with ADHD either treated or not, are law-abiding citizens, with many rising to respected positions as community and business leaders, politicians, athletes, and creative artists.

The Authors
The authors' training and experience make them well equipped to have researched and written this book.

Robert Eme, Ph.D., A.B.P.P. is a board-certified licensed

clinical psychologist and a professor of clinical psychology at Argosy University, Schaumburg, Illinois Campus. For the past 10 years, he has taught future clinical psychologists about ADHD. He specializes in the assessment and treatment of ADHD in his private practice. He is a consultant on ADHD to the Illinois criminal justice system. Dr. Eme's e-mail is **reme@argosyu.edu**

<u>Patrick Hurley</u> has an extensive background in law enforcement and corrections work, as well as an invaluable personal perspective as someone with ADHD. He worked as a law enforcement officer for 17 years, 14 years as a road patrol deputy and sergeant and three as a lieutenant/jail administrator. He also was an adult probation/parole officer for five years. Since being diagnosed with ADHD eight years ago, he has been active in ADHD adult support groups and coaching for ADHD individuals. He is a graduate of the University of Iowa. Mr. Hurley's web site is **http://www.addcorridorcoaching.com** and his e-mail is **addcorridorcoach@aol.com**

SUMMARY

It's estimated that from 30 to 70 percent of inmates may have ADHD.

- One out of three people charged with a crime—and appearing before judges, prosecutors, defense attorneys, jail staff and parole boards—has ADHD.
- A diagnosis of ADHD is not an excuse for law breaking or inappropriate behavior. Yet ADHD is a treatable disorder. By identifying ADHD individuals earlier and improving their quality of life and ability to function, everyone in society benefits.

CHAPTER 1

What is Attention Deficit Hyperactivity Disorder (ADHD)

I magine that you are sitting in a sixth-grade classroom. The teacher is introducing a new chapter in your social studies book. As she begins to read, all you hear is "the ancient Egyptians"because a passing car catches your eye. It's the same color as your Dad's car. It reminds you of the trip you took the day he brought the new car home. A "breaking-in" drive he had called it.

You hear a few more of the teacher's words, "...pyramids as burial...." You recall a movie you saw with pyramids. "King Tut and thieves", she continues. You imagine all the tunnels inside one of the mammoth structures. You see yourself trapped and hear the blocks sliding as they block the exit.

Again, you hear the teacher's voice, "...took hundreds of years...", and you see a calendar with pages flying off into space. Space brings the image of the solar system spinning and asteroids just missing each other.

"...Paying attention? " You realize the teacher is talking to you. In fact, she is standing right beside you, and the class is snickering. Your mind is snapped cruelly back to the classroom. You hadn't realized you'd been so far away.(2)

Each of us has trouble occasionally sitting still, paying attention, or controlling impulsive behavior. For some people, however as the foregoing vignette indicates, those problems prove so pervasive, chronic, and extreme that they interfere with the normal daily activities, including:

- Learning in school
- Holding a job

1

- Maintaining close relationships or raising a family
- Following the rules of society

When symptoms are this extreme, psychology and psychiatry define this condition as a *mental disorder.* Many life-threatening medical disorders are defined as being at an extreme level of symptoms. We're all familiar with the term *hypertension,* for instance. A moderate level of hypertension is not life threatening but, taken to an extreme, it will kill a person. The same extreme level of symptoms characterizes ADHD. In other words, it is the degree to which people with ADHD have trouble sitting still, paying attention, or controlling impulsive behavior that distinguishes them from people without the disorder.(Farone, 2003)

Experts Agree: ADHD Is a Valid Disorder

A remarkable international consensus confirms that ADHD is a real and valid disorder, with characteristic symptoms that can be recognized and treated (Barkley, 2002a). This may come as a revelation to some who recall disagreements throughout the media about the nature of ADHD. *In fact: All major medical associations and government health agencies assert that ADHD is a valid developmental brain disorder.* These agencies include:

- **U.S. Surgeon General**
- **American Medical Association (AMA)**
- **American Psychiatric Association**
- **American Academy of Child and Adolescent Psychiatry (AACAP)**
- **American Psychological Association (APA)**
- **American Academy of Pediatrics (AAP).**

Furthermore, these experts not only recognize ADHD as a valid disorder but also agree that we know a lot about it (Barkley, 2002a).

Now, let's explore brief definitions of terms that will help explain the previous statements.

Valid Disorder

The term *valid disorder* means that overwhelming scientific evidence proves that a set of behaviors exists and causes serious impairments in major life activities such as education, occupational functioning, independent living, and social and family relationships.

We know that ADHD is a valid disorder because scientific evidence has convinced virtually all the experts in the medical, psychiatric, and psychological professions that this indeed is so (Barkley, 2002a, 2003a; Biederman, 2003; Brown, 2003a; Farone, 2003; Newcorn, 2003).

In the words of the commission organized by the American Medical Association in regard to various public concerns regarding ADHD: "ADHD is one of the best researched disorders in medicine, and the overall data on its validity are far more compelling than for most mental disorders and many medical conditions" (Goldman et al., 1998, p. 1105). More than 1,000 scientific articles are published on ADHD every year (Reiff & Tippins, 2004).

This disorder is the most commonly diagnosed behavioral disorder of childhood, occurring in from 6 to 9 percent of the school-aged population (Reiff & Tippins, 2004). Yet, ADHD is not confined to childhood, as its significantly impairing symptoms persist into young adulthood for the majority of children with ADHD (Barkley, 2003a; Farone, 2003; Reiff & Tippins, 2004; Willoughby, 2002).

The Developmental Brain

When we speak of the *developmental brain*, we mean impairment in certain brain functions that one is born with (genetic) and that manifests itself as the individual develops (Barkley, 2003a; Brown, 2003a; Farone, 2003).

Impairment

Impairment means that certain brain functions and, hence, psychological mechanisms are not functioning properly. In our society, many people with these dysfunctions, such as impairments in attention and impulse control, end up in the criminal justice system. Our concern here is why and how professionals in that system can recognize and help these people within our society.

ADHD- Combined Type

There may be a variety of types of ADHD different kinds of ADHD (Barkley, 2003a; Brown, 2003a; Sonuga-Barke, 2002; Todd, Rasmussen, Wood, Levy, & Hay, 2004). The most relevant type/subtype for understanding the criminal offender is called the *combined type*. This type of ADHD is characterized by high levels of inattention, hyperactivity, and impulsivity. The term is included in the standard reference book used by mental health professionals, the *Diagnostic and Statistical Manual of Mental Disorders IV Text Revision* (APA, 2000), or DSM-IV, as it is commonly abbreviated.

For the purposes of this book, the term ADHD will refer to the combined type and not to a type that is predominantly inattentive—that is, a type *without* high levels of hyperactivity and impulsivity. We focus on the combined type because it is much more likely to be associated with behavior that greatly increases the risk for criminal offenses (Barkley, 2003b). We will discuss the predominantly inattentive type of ADHD in Chapter 2, which deals with drug abuse, because this ADHD type may be especially relevant for understanding female drug abusers. Also note that even though the combined type is diagnosed at twice the frequency of the predominantly inattentive type, if all the children in a school system were evaluated, it is likely that the inattentive type would be found to be about 1.5 times as common as the combined type (Reiff & Tippins, 2004).

Core Deficits in ADHD: Inhibition and Attention

Strong scientific consensus points to two main areas of deficit that underlie the central difficulties in ADHD:

- Behavioral inhibition
- Sustained attention.

These deficits manifest in a number of symptoms that can cause struggles in life's everyday activities and therefore increase the risk that a person will engage in antisocial behavior (Barkley, 2002b; Frick & Morris, 2004). Let's look at the particulars for each set of deficits.

Behavioral Inhibition: Overview

I was only nine years old but, boy, do I remember the incident. My father and his friend came back from skin diving and left their spears at the front of the caravan. I grabbed my dad's Hawaiian sling to show cousin Lachlan how it worked, shooting it vertically about ten meters into the air. I repeated this a number of times, until a strong gust of wind blew the spear onto the power lines. It short-circuited the two wires. This happened all in a blink of an eye.

The power pole that Lachlan and I were standing under exploded, with sparks flying everywhere. The current then flowed through all the other poles, blowing them up one after the other in a circle around the caravan park. Every power line connected between the poles fell to the ground, just missing tents and caravans.

People came running to see what had happened. I don't know how it was that no one was killed or injured. The only wires that did not fall were the two with the aluminum spear still lying across them. A State Electricity Commission team arrived to repair the damage.

—(Polis, 2003, p. 34)(3)

Inhibition is the scientific term used to describe the brain's various braking systems (Barkley, 2003b; Nigg, 2001). In ADHD, *behavioral inhibition* refers to the capacity a person has to inhibit or "put a brake on" something he or she is doing or about to do. (Barkley, 2003a). For example, one patient (David, 28) reported that he always had to be doing something and usually something dangerous such as "wheelies" on a motorcycle at 140 mph. He also reported that he could get "real agitated, real quick."

Some individuals with ADHD can be compared to a good car with a faulty brake system. All the other components of their car might be in perfect shape, and their driving skills might be

NASCAR quality. Yet if their brakes are faulty, they can be doing wheelies at 140 mph throughout the course of their lives.

This is essentially what the scientific jargon means when it states that an inhibitory deficit (or *disinhibition*) results in impairment in executive functioning. The term *executive functioning*, while still an evolving concept (Barkley, 2003b; Brown, 2003a), refers to a wide variety of ways in which individuals apply their various skills and abilities to achieve their goals.

In ADHD, incredibly intelligent, talented, and gifted individuals can possess many marvelous abilities and skills. Yet if they also possess a deficit in behavioral inhibition ("braking"), their ability to apply these skills to achieve their life goals is impaired.

This analogy by one of the most prominent experts on ADHD, Thomas Brown (2000, 2003a), should help further clarify this concept: Think of a person with ADHD as an orchestra conductor (the orchestra's "executive"), and think of the orchestra as the total of all his skills and abilities. The person with ADHD may have the best orchestra in the world, but if the conductor is deficient in timing—in other words, deficient in stopping and starting, pausing ("braking")—the coordination and integration of the orchestral instruments will be impaired and the music will be a disaster.

Behavioral Inhibition Symptom: Impulsivity

Even as a young child, I was impulsive and unstoppable. At five, I ran out onto a busy street and was hit by a car, although luckily I wasn't seriously injured.

Later that year, I was burning some trash with my brother. I decided it would be a good idea to burn the frayed white material from the worn-down knees of my jeans. My pants caught fire. I ended up in the hospital with large burn blisters on both legs.

At 14, I was playing with matches and gasoline in our family's two-car detached garage. The gas can suddenly burst into flames, and the garage burned to the ground with my parent's new car inside. My parents somehow believed the story I made up to cover the incident, although the fire department and several of my siblings were suspicious of my tale. Even then, *in early adolescence, I somehow knew that unless I changed my behavior **I** would probably end up in jail someday.*

—Patrick Hurley, co-author

Problems with impulsivity and self-control cause the greatest degree of impairment for all individuals with ADHD (Goldstein, 2003). Deficits in attention receive the most press, but in fact impulsivity is the most important—and most serious—symptom of ADHD.

Because they lack behavioral inhibition, individuals with ADHD often have grave difficulty in stopping themselves from doing things that land them in all sorts of trouble, from injuries to serious antisocial behavior. An inhibitory deficit markedly increases the risk of a person engaging in antisocial behavior. Many with ADHD are prone to act without considering the long-term consequences of their actions. This means that such individuals:

- Act without sufficient reflection
- Get caught up in the heat of the moment
- Are more concerned with the immediate thrill or rewards of their actions than the consequences that might follow
- Only later realize what a mess they have gotten themselves into.

Impulsivity and the Link to Criminal Offending:

- Many offenders with ADHD plan poorly—if at all—before engaging in criminal activity.
- They are more likely to try running from the police. Subsequently, they are more likely to get caught in law-breaking behavior. When arrested, they may be more uncooperative, openly disrespectful, or non-compliant with directives.
- Their behavior tends to be more inconsistent and unpredictable.
- If prone to violent behavior, their actions may be

difficult to anticipate from moment to moment (Goldstein, 1997).

Behavioral Inhibition Symptom: Hyperactivity

Essentially I feel like I need to be in constant motion or I will explode! Overall, it seems my energy level is sometimes inexhaustible. I avoid activities that require me to be quiet. When I participate in activities that do require me to be quiet, it seems like a death sentence to me. I have always been a talker. I can talk about absolutely nothing, with anyone, forever! I have been a chatterbox ever since I was about five. You would think by now I would have run out of things to say.

—young adult female with ADHD

My parents say that I was hyperactive from the day I could walk. I really didn't spend much time crawling. I guess I thought it was too slow. Once I started walking, I got into everything. I'd take stuff out of drawers, closets, cabinets, etc., throw the stuff on the floor, and then move on to the next thing that caught by eye.

When I got a little older, I loved climbing trees. When I wasn't climbing, I was running. My parents had to restrain me in parking lots or street corners, as I would have run out into traffic

—Adult male with ADHD

The term *hyperactivity* refers to excessive or developmentally inappropriate levels of activity that can cause problems for younger children when they are in school or in structured settings where they need to sit quietly. We've all known children who are described as "always on the go; acts if driven by a motor, climbs excessively, can't sit still, talks excessively; is squirmy, fidgety; often hums or makes odd noises" (Barkley, 1998). Some schoolchildren may even go to the extremes of standing on top of their desks, falling out of their chairs, or getting up and wandering around the room.

As the child grows into adolescence and adulthood, these overt levels of hyperactivity may be replaced by more subtle signs, such as constant foot tapping or a pervasive inner restlessness and a great difficulty in relaxing (Wender, 1995). Yet they still have only one gear in their car: fast forward. In addition, when trapped in situations such as boring meetings, those with ADHD may constantly engage in soothing activities such as doodling or they might zone out and be on the verge of falling asleep.

Hyperactivity and the Link to Criminal Offending:

A young person with hyperactivity may jump out of the car when stopped by police, demand to know why he is being stopped, ask a lot of questions, and be either too friendly or overly defensive.

The speech of hyperactive people may appear more rapid than the average person's. Anxiety levels are often higher than what is warranted by the situation.

The hyperactive person may act suspiciously...and appear guilty.

Behavioral Inhibition Symptom: Irritability and Defiance

*Today I am in the U.S. Navy. I have done many stupid things in my career that could have resulted in losing rank or **going to jail**, all because I lost my focus or got bored with the job at hand. Many people thought I was a ticking time bomb waiting to blow. "It's just a matter of time," my boss told me.*

—Young adult male with ADHD(4)

Roger, 35, has been arrested for domestic assault on his wife and resisting arrest. It has taken four officers to arrest and wrestle Roger into the police car and get him to the jail as he has been fighting emotionally and physically the entire way.

Although not appearing to be under the influence of alcohol or drugs, Roger continues to fight and cry as he arrives at the jail. Jail staff immediately assists in escorting Roger to the padded cell. When the door is closed, Roger immediately jumps up and begins screaming and yelling and pounding his fist on the padded walls.

After about an hour, Roger has finally calmed down and jail staff is able to talk to him; he seems fairly calm and rational. Roger agrees

SPINNING OUT OF CONTROL

to undergo the jail booking procedures. During the booking process Roger is still very emotional, crying and apologetic to staff for the way he was acting when he came in. He makes many self-derogatory remarks about how he has messed up his life and hurt his family. Roger presents no further problems to jail staff and after court in the morning is released on his own recognizance.

—From one of Patrick Hurley's cases

In short, individuals with ADHD have difficulty controlling, regulating, inhibiting, or putting a brake on emotions (Barkley, 2003b; Wender, 1995). Their behavior can be irritable, excitable, intolerant of stress, and explosive. The explosive, hot temper proves the most worrisome behavior.

Interestingly, with ADHD, what distinguishes this explosive behavior is that it is typically short lived. The person cools off quickly, does not brood, and then wonders why those who have been exposed to the explosiveness have not recovered as quickly (Wender, 1995)

<u>Irritability and Defiance and the Link to Criminal Offending:</u>
- Having a short fuse or low boiling-point is a recipe for disastrous relationships, especially those involving authority.
- Individuals with ADHD are often more argumentative or defiant—especially with parents, teachers, police, and other authority figures. Therefore, it becomes more likely that these individuals will be in more frequent contact with the criminal justice system.
- Run-ins and conflicts with authority figures can give a person a reputation for being antisocial. These people often experience trouble with getting or keeping a job.
- They have many conflicts with supervisors at work, become quickly bored, and pigeonhole themselves

into minimum wage jobs—all they or outsiders view them as qualified for.

Joe, an 18-year-old with a poor driving record, is well-known to local law enforcement officers. He actually has charges of driving without a license dating back to age 14, and his license has been suspended on several occasions. He has just gone through a posted 25 mile-per-hour speed zone driving 38 miles per hour; an officer has detected him on radar.

Joe got his license reinstated only three days ago and now knows he is about to be stopped again. The officer may or may not know about Joe and his past problems. When the officer makes the stop, Joe jumps out of his vehicle and comes toward the officer with an angry look on his face. The officer, who does not know Joe, tells him to get back into his vehicle. Joe, with disgust on his face, complies

The officer making the stop has viewed Joe already in an unfavorable light, and Joe's odds for a negative outcome in this traffic stop have increased tremendously even though the situation did not escalate.

—one of Patrick Hurley's cases

Attention: Overview

I have had this problem all my life. I often find myself 20 or 30 pages into a book before realizing that my mind has been elsewhere since page 10. With force, I can overcome this briefly, but the effort exhausts me. I usually give up and move on to something else

—Young adult male with ADHD

The problem that dominated my life and shaped my personality was the need to avoid the piercing, rasping, blasting, disorganized chaos of incoming stimuli that I could not filter out, could not ignore. This made it hard for me to relate to other people; to think, study, make it in school, to carry out tasks, plan ahead, and remember.

– Young adult male with ADHD

The term *attention* refers to a complex process or set of processes that can be subdivided into a number of distinct functions (Mirsky & Duncan, 2003). Two of the most important functions for understanding criminal offenders are *sustained attention* and *selective attention* (also called *focused attention)*.

Sustained Attention: Staying On Task

My skin crawls when I have to sit down and study boring material. After 3 or 4 minutes, I will tune out or fall asleep. It requires tremendous energy to stay focused. Consequently I am a "deadly procrastinator."

– Young adult male

In my own personal experience, I suffered greatly throughout my education. I recall feeling frustrated since grade school. My boredom got the best of me; therefore, I began to dream. I believe boredom is tied to ADHD in that the person with ADHD learns to adapt to under-stimulation by engaging in fantasy as a way of creating stimulation

—25-year-old female with a Psy.D. in Psychology

"Sustained attention" is the ability to stay on task and pay attention, especially to those activities that are repetitive, effortful, uninteresting, or are chosen for the individual by someone else. The classic example is that of homework. In most cases, dull or boring homework for some individuals with ADHD is never done, only partially done, done only when a parent constantly flogs the person to do so, or done only at the last minute in a rushed haphazard dash to the finish.

Yet in tasks they find interesting, persons with ADHD can sustain attention for hours; a young person with ADHD can play video games forever! Most individuals with ADHD have a few activities where attention impairments are absent, which may make ADHD look like a willpower problem, a problem of simple laziness (Barkley, 1998; Brown, 2003a). **It is not** (Brown, 2003a).

We know what you're thinking: "Well, no one likes to do homework anyway, but they do it if they want to do well in school and if they're self-disciplined." That might be true for most people but not for people with significant deficits in attention. When faced with work that is boring or repetitive, their brains can actually "shut down" and not much they can voluntarily do will re-open it.

Here is where we ask the reader to pay close attention to the single most damaging misunderstanding of ADHD: People with ADHD can pay attention if they want to. To the uninitiated, it might seem that way. Yet the fact is, just because individuals with ADHD can display an incredible variability does not mean they are any more lazy, irresponsible, or unmotivated than the person without ADHD. It is because *their brains **cannot** sustain attention in circumstances that they find tedious, dull, or boring.*

It's a Matter of "Can't" Rather Than "Won't"

Studies of individuals with and without ADHD illustrate the differences in brain patterns that distinguish the brains of the two groups. When faced with a tedious, dull, boring task, the brain regions engaged by the task of those *without* ADHD remain awake, aroused, and activated, whereas these same brain regions of those with ADHD are under-aroused and under-activated (Barkley, 2002b; Loo, 2004; Monastra, 2004; Pliszka, 2002).

We'll explain the reasons for this under-activation later in the book, when we discuss the causes of ADHD. For now, the message is simply this:

Most people can make themselves sustain attention to boring tasks. Those with ADHD are gravely impaired in sustaining attention because the brain regions that should enable them to do so are impaired. ADHD is a disorder of brain impairment, not a disorder of laziness or will power.

Try this analogy. You are very fatigued, but you must continue to read this book, do your homework, and pay the bills. Certainly, you can vigorously and earnestly struggle against sleepiness and complete the task at hand. It will take a great deal more effort and more time than if you were rested and alert, but it is doable. Now imagine spending your entire life having to intensely struggle to sustain attention to the numerous tasks that you do not find invigorating. You would be at high risk for developing the unsavory reputation of a lazy, irresponsible, and unmotivated so-and-so. Welcome to the world of ADHD!

Finally, note that impairments in sustained attention may also be due in part to deficits in what is termed "working memory" (Barkley, 2003a).

Sustained Attention Factor: Working Memory

Many times, written and oral instructions are not clear to those of us who have ADHD. An instruction that seems simple for you to understand may contain a phrase that confuses me. The instructions may have too much information for us to absorb and file away. We need to have each step of a job explained in detail.

—Young adult female with ADHD

Let's draw once again on the car analogy. When driving along city streets and trying to locate a particular address, the driver must focus on important information: stoplights, another car veering into the lane, or the addresses on the respective houses. At the same time, the driver must ignore irrelevant information, such as what is playing on the radio. The ability that will help the driver find the address without getting lost or crashing (Baddely, 2001; Mackintosh & Bennett, 2003) is called *working memory*—that ability to temporarily store and organize relevant information

Here's another example: Can you solve a mental math problem? If so, you solved it because, in part, you were able to keep the relevant math information on line, organize it, and manipulate it to solve the problem. Let's apply working memory to the spinning top metaphor. Think of working memory as the map the top needs to successfully navigate and cruise the tabletop. If the map cannot be accurately remembered, cruising quickly becomes careening—and crashing.

Joe, our 18-year-old driver stopped for speeding, may have been trying to watch his speed since getting his license back recently; he wanted to avoid any more tickets. He may have even been proud of himself for driving so carefully.

Joe is a senior at the local high school and in the last class of the day received a low grade on the test he had taken last week; he is upset. While driving home, he lets his mind wander (like many other individuals do) and, in just a few minutes, went from driving 40 miles per hour in a 45 zone to driving 38 miles per hour in a 25 mile per hour zone. His frustration with being stopped is more (ongoing) disappointment in himself than anger at the officer for stopping him. Unfortunately, the officer knows nothing about Joe, his difficulty at school, or even his problem driving record as yet. He will soon find out about the driving record from his dispatcher.

It's not a large leap, then, to understanding the role working memory plays in sustaining attention. If one is to stay on task, it is important to remember the goal or goals that the task or activity is meant to achieve. Remembrance of the goal puts the memory to work in reviving and nourishing motivation to persist in a task, even if there is no immediate gratification

Sustained Attention Deficits and the Link to Criminal Offending

What then is the relevance of impairments in sustaining attention and working memory in understanding the criminal offender? The five most important implications, reviewed in the following sections, are:
- Academic failure
- Work failure
- Forgetfulness
- Impaired sense of time
- Failure to learn from the past
- Failure to plan for the future.

Attention Factor: Academic Failure
When Jack Sanders was growing up, he didn't know he had an

attention deficit disorder. All he knew was that he had an excess of energy, a talent for getting into trouble, and a brain that, from time to time, would inexplicably go on strike.

He chafed under authority, often resolving conflicts with his mouth and fists. He attended five Chicago high schools (one stint lasted a mere six hours) before he finally earned a diploma(5)

(Note that Mr. Sanders subsequently made millions in the trading pits of the Chicago Mercantile Exchange, where he also served as chairman for an unprecedented 17 years.)

ADHD may predispose a child to academic failure in two major ways. First, it contributes to a greater risk of developing behavior problems that reduce academic performance. Second, even in those who are motivated to do well in school, impaired working memory can cause grave academic difficulties. These difficulties increase the likelihood that the student will reject the socializing school experience for more frisky antisocial street experiences. Thus, even very bright, highly motivated individuals with ADHD can have the following academic difficulties (Barkley, 2003b; Dendy, 2002):

- Remembering and following directions.
- Retrieving information for an exam (even when they studied diligently).
- Memorizing math facts, spelling words, and dates.
- Performing mental math computation that involves remembering one part of a problem while working on another.
- Coherently summarizing and organizing what has been read.

Multiple-choice exams can be especially troublesome because they require exactly recalling specific information while keeping in mind the multiple-choice question as well as the four or five possible choices. Essay exams are typically easier if students can get away with simply throwing everything they can remember into a heap.

If the teacher requires coherence and organization, the essays can be failures.

All the foregoing difficulties can converge to produce a perfect storm that may be devastating to self-esteem. In childhood, however, many appear to cope with these academic, as well as social and behavioral difficulties, by viewing themselves as functioning at a higher level than they actually are (Hoza et al., 2004). For others, and especially for those who have already developed some symptoms of depression, the perfect storm helps to explain why from 45 to 59 percent of those with ADHD eventually develop an anxiety or depressive disorder (Brown, 2004b).

A Personal Account from Co-Author Patrick Hurley

Consider the following first-person account of co-author Patrick Hurley, who explains how the roots of poor self-esteem begin in childhood for many with ADHD and continue into adulthood.

Self-esteem, or rather struggling with it, is a common problem for persons with ADHD. This can usually be traced back to events of childhood where there was a struggle to cope with everyday problems that other kids handled much easier.

Stress also came from parents, teachers, and friends who would see us doing well in one subject and completely failing another subject. Often, we were bright, and so poor performance was attributed to lack of motivation or not working up to potential... My report cards were full of comments to this effect.

We youngsters with ADHD may have been able to recite every commercial jingle from television ads and the theme song to every popular television show, but asking us to do a word math problem or get our multiplication tables down seemed like asking us to cross the ocean without a boat. If parents, teachers, and friends didn't understand these discrepancies, they could join the club, because we didn't understand either.

Believe me, as a young child, I wanted in the worst way to fit in and be normal, and I imagine other children do, too. The effort and time it takes to deal with the fact that we don't fit in far exceeds the effort and time it *would for us to succeed in fitting in. In other words, <u>it's harder to not fit in than to fit in.</u>*

Many of us were blamed for lack of willpower and accused of being "lazy and not caring. " Yet, this was exactly the opposite of what we wanted to be. We just couldn't seem to show this to anyone. Their criticisms of us seemed valid when we honestly looked at ourselves. We may have tried to overcome them and still had problems.

At any rate, over time we validated others' claims and our own feelings of being lazy, uncaring, and lacking in willpower. Couple these with other problems such as blurting out whatever might come to our mind—like telling our best friend "you have bad breath"—and the result is another lost friendship, another person mad at us, and another person who will probably gossip about us. In other words: more isolation and the loss of even more self-esteem.

If we remained quiet in class, that was viewed negatively. If we thought we knew the answer and blurted it out before anyone else could, so that the teacher knew we knew, that didn't work, either. If we tried raising our hand, waving it violently and biting our tongue to keep from blurting out the answer, the teacher called on someone else. If we spoke up in class, it was probably in excess and that wasn't good. Somehow, everything we tried was unacceptable

All of this we carried with us as we matured through adolescence and into adulthood. Many of us continued to beat up ourselves inside. Others went down the path of blaming everyone else for all their problems, becoming oppositional and difficult and rejecting anyone and everyone in authority.

Patrick Hurley's experience is typical. Still, just because a child does well academically does not mean the child is not suffering from ADHD deficits. Academic difficulties might be minimal for some children who are very bright or who attend schools that advocate minimalist academic expectations. In addition, highly motivated individuals, especially females, may not show obvious problems because they compensate for working memory impairments by studying longer and harder.

Attention Factor: Work Failure

*When **Vivienne Sales** finally broke her silence, she did so loudly, losing her temper in the hushed library where she worked. It was August 2003, and she had been hanging on to her job as a reference librarian by the most fragile of threads. For more than a year her supervisors at the Embry-Riddle Aeronautical University in Prescott, Ariz., had been warning her that she was sometimes sloppy and inaccurate. She was late for work too often, they said. She didn't dress neatly and appropriately. Her desk was always a mess.*

Sales knew all this. She also knew why. Three years earlier, when she was 36, she was told she had attention-deficit hyperactivity disorder. The news was a relief because it seemed to explain everything—why she rarely seemed to fit into a workplace, why she left nine different jobs in 1999 alone, why, despite two master's degrees and years of dogged hard work, she never seemed to get anywhere.(6)

__Carl Mandiola__ is 37 and he can list more than 50 jobs that he has run through in his working life. He has tended bar, served in the Air Force and been an emergency room technician. He has sold Amway products, waterbeds, cookies, shoes and long-distance phone service. He has worked security at a supermarket, been a janitor in a medical lab, made pizza at a fast-food joint and assembled butyl rubber innards for compression tanks on a factory line. In all, he has been fired from a dozen jobs for poor performance and from a half-dozen more because he was downsized, and he left the rest because he became antsy and bored.

"Most people cannot believe that someone with three university degrees could be such a washout in the real world."

The same difficulties that contribute to academic failure, as well as others that will be discussed shortly, can contribute to disastrous work failures in many occupations as the preceding vignettes illustrated. As a result of poor performance, boredom and impulsivity, adults with ADHD have more frequent job changes, are less likely to be employed, and more likely to be under employed. (Belkin, 2004).

However, once again note that as with school work, there is tremendous variability in job performance, depending upon the kind of work involved. Work that is dull, repetitive, stationary, loaded with detailed paperwork, requiring organized multitasking, etc. are deadly nightmares. For example, a social work position that requires the accurate completion of several detail besotted forms in a timely manner is a recipe for disaster.

On the other hand, work that involves a lot of movement, chatting, excitement, frequent changes, etc. can be performed at a high level. Examples of such jobs include: sales, waitressing, hairdressing, stock trading, acting, law enforcement, emergency medicine, etc.

Furthermore, in some instances, ADHD can be harnessed as an asset. For example, recall the prior vignette of Jack Sanders who parleyed his high energy, impulsivity and risk taking in millions. Similarly, Thomas Apple who was diagnosed with ADHD in his early 40's, went on to create the largest video display for stock market quotations. He asserts that ADHD is *the source of my creativity. You can think outside of the box because you are not in a box."* (Belkin, 2004, p. 54).

Attention Factor: Forgetfulness

*As a child and adolescent I'd forget assignments, appointments, information people told me. This is still true of me today. People have to remind me often to do things. For this reason my wife pays the bills. Most of the time, when I lose something it is due to forgetting where I put it. Or I can't find it in my **piles of stuff.***

— Young adult male with ADHD

Forgetfulness in ADHD is genuine, not just a cop out. Forgetfulness contributes not only to numerous academic difficulties such as forgetting to take homework to school (when it has actually been completed) but also to failing to keep appointments or arrive on time and difficulty meeting life obligations that typically involve balancing several simultaneous tasks.

ADHD AND THE CRIMINAL JUSTICE SYSTEM

Consider the following invitation to disaster: Ask a child with ADHD to use her automatic pilot to get going in the morning so she can actually arrive at school on time with all her stuff. She may have to remember to set her alarm to awaken, get up when it goes off, make breakfast, brush teeth, put clothes on, gather school supplies and books, take lunch, walk the dog—the list seems endless. Without constant parental guidance (nagging), this child will wobble all over the house, perhaps disengaging altogether as she cuddles up with a toy that has attracted her attention.

Imagine this stress and disability magnified throughout a lifetime as the person enters the job market, marries, tries to maintain a social life, and pays bills. The person with ADHD frequently becomes known as lazy, lying, irresponsible, and stupid. From there, it is but a small step from being labeled culpable and hopelessly irresponsible to deciding to accept the labels. The child grows into a young adult who has assumed a negative, criminal identity.

Attention Factor: Sense of Time
At the heart of ADHD is a relativistic perception of time:

Time has never stopped seeming as elastic and deceptive to me as it was when I was six years old; the bell has always rung too soon, the car rides always take too long.

For me, and I suspect for others like me, there is no sense of a continuous whole against which to measure the parts. It is a child's sense of time. Everything must be done or said now. In short there is only now and not now.

The absence of an inner sense of time makes every change in the emotional climate seem permanent thereby creating large, sudden swings in mood.

—Adult male with ADHD(7)

Given a deficit in working memory, individuals with ADHD have a specific time impairment that extends beyond

21

simple forgetfulness. Hence, individuals with ADHD often have difficulty:

- Holding events in mind
- Using their sense of time to prepare for upcoming events
- Judging the passage of time
- Accurately estimating how much time it will take to finish a task
- Learning from the past and planning for the future (Dendy, 2002).

Criminal-justice professionals will recognize the chronic criminal offender in all these examples. Recognizing, however, is not always understanding. It is critical to remember that in offenders with ADHD these failures are in part due to a cognitive deficit and not solely due to bad attitude. Impaired working-memory means that the individual is less capable of accessing and keeping the past on line as well as less capable of extending time into the future. As one client with ADHD put it, "There is only now and not now." In short, the ability to plan, even in the presence of adequate to high intelligence, is impaired.

Selective Attention: Avoiding Distractions

"Spinning" is an interesting word to describe my ADHD mind. It never stops spinning. At times, it spins so fast that I have to stop what I am doing and just watch. I imagine I'm looking inside of my head, and I see a picture very similar to a spinning galaxy in space. The only difference is that the galaxy in my mind spins much faster. I see thousands of colored dots in a pattern, all turning the same direction. I am so hypnotized by this picture that I hear nothing but the whir of the thoughts flying randomly within my brain. If I am lucky, one of these thoughts will be the one I need at the moment.

—Young adult male with ADHD

Selective (also called *focused*) attention refers to the ability to stay on a task without becoming distracted by internal or external stimuli. At any moment in daily life, any of us can be bombarded by an array of internal and external stimuli—while we are expected to remain focused on a job at hand: a conversation, a meeting, a book, a project. We have to ignore the outside stimuli if we are to function effectively.

Although some scientists maintain that this type of attention deficit is not a core problem in ADHD (Sandberg, 2002), there are an enormous number of clinical vignettes in which individuals describe this as a core deficit. Many people with ADHD report grave difficulty in staying focused because they are bombarded by a buzzing, blooming profusion of inner and outer stimuli. In other words, they experience stimulus overload because they cannot inhibit or put a brake on this bombardment. Witness the following:

In one of my earliest memories, I was about three years old lying on my bed, eyes closed, rocking my head back and forth, and groaning "ah, ah, ah" with each movement—a kind of ritual chant to hold at bay the clamor of sounds making it impossible for me to go to sleep. Ordinary sounds. My twin brother, Dan, breathing in sleep in the bed next to mine. The radio playing in the living room. A dog barking. Everyday sounds unbearably amplified in my mind.

I just knew that rocking my head back and forth on the pillow and making the groaning noise helped to deaden the other noises that were beating at me, the overwhelming bombardment of sensations that didn't seem to bother other people but were painful for me. The problem that dominated my life and shaped my personality was the need to avoid the piercing, rasping, blasting, disorganized chaos of incoming stimuli that 1 could not filter out, could not ignore.

My sensitivity to all stimuli increased as I grew older. Indoors or out, the space around me seemed flooded with sounds that were too loud, lights and colors that were too bright, odors that were too intense, tastes that were too strong, touches that were too harsh. I could not shut them out. They were piercing and confusing.

—*Overload!* (Miller & Blum, 1996, p. 23).

Attention Deficits and the Link to Criminal Offending:

Inattentiveness may not be readily apparent with initial police contact. This may be seen during interrogations, interviews, or court appearances when the person does not respond to questions and requests. Those with ADHD may miss questions, ask the police officer, attorney, or judge to repeat the question, appear to be daydreaming, appear unconcerned or uncooperative. They may appear restless or impatient.

Example:

Jim is a 32-year-old man arrested overnight for a third offense driving under the influence of alcohol. He has sobered up before his court appearance in front of the judge in the morning and has had a chance to assess his situation. He realizes the problems he is facing with not only the law but also with his wife and family, his work, and his finances. He has been through alcohol substance abuse treatment before and knows he will have to do more.

In front of the judge he pleads not guilty, and the judge is telling him a number of things of importance that Jim should be totally focused on. Among these are reporting to the probation office as a term of pre-trial release supervision that has been imposed on him, going to a substance abuse treatment facility for an updated substance abuse evaluation, not driving, and attending upcoming court dates. The judge hands him a stack of documents, which Jim takes from him.

The problem is that Jim has been trying to listen and think about his mess at the same time. Even though the information is written down for him to look at later, Jim heard little of what the judge has explained to him and fails to follow up on the substance abuse evaluation or reporting to the probation officer for pre-trial supervision. He gets released from jail and sets an appointment with his usual lawyer for two weeks down the road. By the time he meets with his lawyer, who asks if he has reported to the probation officer or gotten his substance abuse evaluation, Jim is probably already in even more trouble.

—From one of Patrick Hurley's cases

Attention Factor: Organizational Skills

Most individuals with ADHD have difficulties organizing in most areas of their lives. Some may develop compulsive coping strategies, such as tons of reminder lists. At the basic level of stuff, their rooms, desks at school, or cars can resemble expanses of flotsam, several fathoms deep. At the cognitive level, their written work can resemble dream reveries, connected by random associations that even Freud would have difficulty decoding. At the level where they have to function at the speed of life, they have difficulties simultaneously coordinating several activities.

There are three major reasons for this chaos (Kohlberg, 2002):

Distractibility. Organization requires attentiveness, a concentrated focus over time to get the job done. ADHD's hallmark symptom of distractibility is diametrically opposed to achieving this goal.

Boredom. There can be nothing more mind numbing and spirit killing than having to tediously, patiently sustain attention to innumerable trivial stimuli to achieve a reasonable facsimile of organization. The ADHD brain is terminally opposed to such endeavors!

Out of sight, out of mind. People need to remember to do things that are not right in front of their nose. Individuals with ADHD have an impaired working memory. Their memory can be perfect, but they have difficulty putting it to work. Think of memory as a mailbox. People with ADHD can have as big a mailbox as anyone else has, but they forget to retrieve the mail.

Organizational Deficits and the Link to Criminal Offending:

- Persons with ADHD often lack organization skills, fail to keep appointments, and procrastinate chronically.
- They seem unable to set priorities, leading to a lack of achievement and productivity.
- They can appear indifferent to requirements and rules placed on them by their parents or teachers or by police, attorneys, parole officers, or judges.

Related Core Deficits: Social Skills

Sometimes I act really goofy. Last week I was squawking like a chicken. My friends ask me why I am so hyper. They tease me about being weird, hyperactive, and crazy. I have mood swings and then get into fights with my friends

—Female with ADHD

Beth is an eight-year-old second grader. Although seen as intelligent, Beth has trouble completing assigned tasks in a timely fashion. Her social skills are poor and she has a tendency to say what is on her mind, which has cost her more friendships than she can recall. She is easily distracted in class, and the teacher often calls on her, knowing that she does not seem to be paying attention. This causes her classmates to label Beth as "stupid." With few friends, she finds herself isolated and defensive and calls herself the "cootie girl" that no one wants to associate with. This can turn sour quickly and result in frustration that is seen as aggressive, disrespectful, and insensitive. It all adds up to trouble for Beth at an early age and a continued decline in her self-esteem.

—Female with ADHD

Inattentiveness, impulsivity, hyperactivity, and emotional over-responsiveness result in significant problems in peer relationships for the majority of children with ADHD (Barkley, 1998). These deficits can mean that children with ADHD are more likely to be:

- **Aggressive**
- **Stubborn**
- **Disruptive**
- **Domineering**
- **Bossy**
- **Noisy**
- **Insensitive to another's viewpoint**
- **Narcissistic**

In adulthood and especially in intimate relationships such as marriage, social problems take the form of zoning out, blowing out, and copping out (Robin, 2001).

- *Zoning out* refers to difficulty in listening, becoming distracted while doing tasks, not really noticing what is going on with the other person, and being chronically disorganized and easily overwhelmed.
- *Blowing out* refers to impulsive emotional outbursts in word and deed, which can occur over even minor life events.
- *Copping out* refers to difficulty in completing projects, sticking to plans, remembering things, fulfilling commitments, getting to places on time, attending to details, and generally planning and organizing work and family life.

These impairments in adults also can result in deficient parenting, where there are special difficulties in being consistent, and in maintaining attention to supervising and monitoring children (Weiss, Hechtman, & Weiss, 2000).

Many persons with ADHD come from families in which the inherited condition is fairly common and often results in unstable or dysfunctional family relationships. In fact, in some families, the disorder may be so prevalent that a person who does not exhibit this condition may actually be considered the "abnormal" one in the family. These "abnormal" family members may go on to become successful despite their apparent dysfunctional family background. These successful family members sometimes intentionally distance themselves from their families to escape patterns that may date back for many generations.

On the other hand, some ADHD individuals come from highly functional families and stand out in a negative way from their successful siblings. Family members can be frustrated with this individual and can relate a litany of problems the afflicted family member has displayed over the years. Still others with ADHD can be such good actors that family members may be surprised by the action that has gotten the individual in trouble.

<u>Social Skills Deficits and the Link to Criminal Offending:</u>
- Persons with ADHD involved in lawbreaking behavior are often co-defendants with other dysfunctional individuals. That is because they seem to attract others who are impulsive and have the same features of reckless and antisocial behavior.
- Their co-defendants are probably either dominant criminal types who are more devious and use their ADHD acquaintances to do the dirty work or other ADHD persons with whom they relate well.
- Fortunately for society, persons with ADHD often make inept criminals and are usually caught by tripping themselves up with poor planning, easily contradicted statements, or outright confessions of their illegal activities. They often make the error of bragging about their exploits to others.

A Word about Gender Differences

Scientific agreement shows that boys are about three times more likely to be diagnosed with ADHD than are girls (Reiff & Tippins, 2004). Beyond this basic agreement, however, there is a vigorous debate among the experts regarding whether or not the sexes differ in the nature of their ADHD (Barkley, 2003a; Goldstein & Gordon, 2003; Quinn & Nadeau, 2002).

For our purposes, we can bypass much of the debate because our focus is on how females with ADHD (with high levels of symptoms of disinhibition) would present in the criminal justice system as opposed to the community in general. And, it is clear that such females with ADHD demonstrate the same core symptoms as do males (Barkley, 2003b Goldstein & Gordon, 2003), with much the same pattern of impairment. Thus, though gender may modify the symptom expression somewhat—such as impulsivity being expressed as sexual promiscuity or hyperactivity being manifested as non-stop chatter as opposed to disruptive class clowning, etc.—

the foregoing discussion of the core symptoms, disinhibition and inattention, is equally applicable to both males and females.

Finally, one extremely important gender difference stands out, and its relevance especially applies to the area of drug abuse. Namely, although the combined type of ADHD (high levels of inattention as well as over-activity and impulsivity) is diagnosed about 250 percent more often in boys than in girls; the predominantly inattentive type is probably 150 percent more common than the combined type. Furthermore, and most importantly, girls are more likely to have the predominantly inattentive type than boys are (Reiff & Tippins, 2004).

SUMMARY

Two main deficits explain the central difficulties that many people with ADHD experience: behavioral inhibition and sustained attention. These deficits can contribute to criminal-offending behavior in a variety of ways.

- In general, *behavioral inhibition* deficits cause a person to be more prone to impulsivity, hyperactivity, irritability, and defiance.
- We say that people with ADHD often have problems "putting on the brakes" to their behavior. In other words, these individuals have more trouble with acting impulsively (without thinking through consequences), being constantly restless, and having a short fuse, especially when it comes to authority figures.
- *Attention deficits* mean the person can have difficulty staying on task and paying attention.
- These attention deficits manifest in a number of symptoms that can cause struggles in everyday life activities and therefore increase the risk that a person will engage in antisocial behavior.
- These deficits include getting easily sidetracked

from goals and objectives, being unable to tune out distractions, losing track of time, failing in school, and lacking the social skills that can provide a strong social network.

CHAPTER 2
ADHD and Increased Risk of Antisocial Behavior

The previous chapter presented numerous examples of how the core deficits in ADHD increased the risk for developing anti-social behavior. This chapter will build upon that discussion by presenting detailed case history as well as the formal scientific theory that seeks to explain how increased risk is translated into antisocial behavior.

We begin with Part I, the case history of David. He was chronically dysfunctional, highly intelligent, and a few months away from his 26th birthday when he was evaluated for ADHD by co-author Robert Eme, Ph.D. At that time, David's mother predicted that her son "is either going to be in jail or dead by the time he is 26." Four years subsequent to this dire prediction, David was flourishing in virtually all aspects of his life.

This case history relates how this remarkable recovery took place and provides an example of what can happen for the many other "Davids" and their female counterparts with ADHD who are either in the criminal justice system or likely to find themselves there unless they are diagnosed and receive good treatment.

Part II of this chapter examines the "gene-environment interaction theory." This crucial theory states that genetically influenced individual differences interact with certain environmental characteristics to produce pathology, including ADHD.

Part I: David's Story

David's Development

As presented in his mother's words, David's development exhibited the classic symptoms of ADHD:

David was often infuriating as a child. If I asked him to do something, he'd go off to do it, but when I'd turn around to check, it wouldn't be done and he'd be doing something else. His room was always a wreck. When asked to clean it (rather, organize it—pick up things, put them in their places, etc.) he'd start to. I'd poke my head in a while later and he'd be playing with a toy or involved in something else, his room pretty much as it had been. It seemed that organizing his room was just too big a job for David to do. So, I'd help him.

Everything was a big deal to get done. I'd be exasperated trying to get him ready for school on time. He'd start to get ready and then would be off doing something else when it was time to go. I felt caught between David and his stepfather, Jack, for example, when he would ask David to do something and it would never happen.

David's IQ is very high and so he could do quite well at school, except he didn't. Schoolwork was boring. Projects weren't completed. So, he'd have a "D" or an "F," and then he'd ace the final. He knew the material. It was just boring putting it down on paper. And, he lost things at school, like his notebook and his homework. He was so disorganized. I bought him organizers for his school things, a notebook in which to write down assignments and due dates. Nothing helped. He didn't seem to care.

The school realized suddenly as a result of testing that David was "gifted" and put him in their gifted program. Then I'd get calls that David wasn't completing the assignments required by the gifted program and was on the verge of being dropped from the program. Jack and I went to a meeting one evening for parents of gifted children. We were asked, "Is your child's room messy? Does your child switch from one subject to another, not completing tasks?" It was explained, "Your child behaves this way because your child is gifted." After so much frustration and misunderstanding, we finally had an answer, something to hold on to that could help us understand David—except that it didn't help David or us.

Socially, David just didn't fit in with others. I'd sit at the window, watching children walking home from school in twos and threes. David walked alone. While other children played outside together in the summer, David played or watched television alone. In his teens David made the one friend he has to this day. He became more sociable and had girlfriends and other friends—but they didn't seem to last.

David as a Teenager: Suicide Attempts

David's mother continues with her recollection of David's development into adolescence:

David's self-esteem was very low. As a youngster he talked about dying. In his teens he attempted suicide by taking over-the-counter sleeping medication and was twice treated in psychiatric hospitals with no positive results. David's situation worsened.

David was an angry young man and tension was high between him and Jack—and me. I couldn't understand why my gifted son couldn't "get his act together." He became extremely aggressive at home to the point where police intervention was required. He was asked to leave home at the age of 18.

He lived in California with my brother until, after several suicide threats; he came home to find David sitting in the living room, holding a wine glass filled with Liquid-Plummer. David returned to his home state, lived with his girlfriend, had a son, and married. Then his wife left him and his infant son. David attempted suicide by taking an overdose of Tylenol. He lost one job, started another, and lost it because he couldn't handle "down time" when working as a radio dispatcher. He'd have what he described as panic attacks. Social relationships were a problem, starting out intense and then dissolving into misunderstanding and conflict. David didn't understand why girlfriends ended their relationships with him.

David lost his apartment, lost his car, couldn't support his son, and slept on the couch in his friend's apartment until he could no longer stay there. David told me that he was disintegrating and that he was making plans for his funeral. He then moved in with his stepfather and me.

David complained of "panic attacks" and "heart problems," reporting that his heart had stopped several times (he had previously gone to the ER by ambulance because of these feelings). His first day with us he had an "attack," which appeared to be shortness of breath as he held his chest gasping. I called the doctor, but David said he was "fine now." Two short psych tests (that I administered) suggested malingering. I took David to a heart specialist. No abnormalities were found. Since he had no job and no money, I suggested he go to Family Services for therapy (they have a sliding scale). The psychiatrist suspected, based on David's verbalized symptoms, a seizure disorder and suggested neurological testing, which David could not afford.

Back Home and Sliding Fast

David's mother explains how she and her husband struggled to make sense of David's behavior after he returned home to live:

At home for the first time in years, our adult son's behaviors were shocking. His room was such a mess that there was no clear floor space on which to walk to put a telephone message on his nightstand. I'd step on papers on the floor and then hear the crack of a tape underneath. Layers of things covered the floor, including money and dirty dishes. His bed was never made. Important items were lost in there but he refused to clean it up.

When Jack asked David to input data on his computer, David couldn't do it—making mistake after mistake. Then he'd go upstairs and sit at his computer for five or six hours at a time playing games—doing things he wanted to do. So Jack declared David to be lazy and selfish. David lost keys, papers, and phone numbers that were very important to him. He left on a trip to Connecticut with a friend without enough money to make it back home.

I knew something was really wrong but couldn't figure out what it was. For example, why would a 25-year-old young man who had a child, didn't have a job, or a real plan for getting a job or an apartment, even though he had a deadline for how long he could live with us, sit for six hours at a stretch at his computer and then go out drinking with friends?

David always had an answer, however, for anyone who asked about his plans. He was going to California in August to live and go to school. Except, he had no money to do this and no plans or apparent inclination to work. He wasn't realistic. Although his "health problems" decreased without reinforcement, he was in limbo and not functioning competently, apparently not "able" to be self-sufficient. I was afraid that when David left us he would be unable to keep things "together," go downhill, and would wind up homeless, hospitalized, in jail, or dead.

Finally: David's Diagnosis

David's mother continues with the story of how she learned that ADHD could explain many of her son's problems:

Then, I was in an "Eme" class (authors' note: the mother was a student of co-author Robert Eme), listening to a lecture on ADHD. I'd completed my readings and had listened intently throughout the lecture. However, it wasn't until the last few minutes of class that it hit me like a lightening bolt—ADHD was David's problem! It explained so much of David's troubles. And while I thought it might not be the total "answer," I believed that it was the foundation upon which David's "out of control" life had been built. The whole drive home from school my heart was in my throat. I arrived home, dragged David off his computer and said, "David, I think I know what the problem is."

The formal diagnostic evaluation was conducted shortly thereafter and a regimen of stimulant medication was begun. Note that there was not any other form of intervention other than medication. David was resistant, probably because his experience of about two decades of intermittent psychotherapy, which had been utterly worthless, left him feeling highly skeptical.

David Four Years into Treatment: A New Life

Recall that at the time of the diagnosis, David's chronically dysfunctional life was on the verge of culminating in jail and/or death. The situation was essentially hopeless despite numerous prior intensive interventions that were oblivious to the existence of the disorder. In the words of David's mother.

Prior to David's diagnosis of ADHD, I believed that David's future was bleak, that he would probably spend his days depressed and dependent upon others, unable to eke out a living for himself and his young son. David saw only a downhill course and talked often of death. Then David was correctly diagnosed and treated with Ritalin.

Two years later he is well, functioning in work and in his personal/ interpersonal life. He is happy, often euphoric, with a delightful sense of humor; his cup is always half full. This description of a 27- year-old man may be typical of many middle-class young adults in the mid-1990s. For me, however, David's mother, this description of David's current level and quality of functioning is akin to a miracle. David is alive and well, with a positive attitude and a bright future. I believe that this would not have been possible without an accurate diagnosis of ADHD and appropriate treatment.

David's ADHD, which now appears to have been so obvious, had been missed completely by mental health practitioners (psychotherapists, psychologists, and psychiatrists) who had assessed and treated David in his teens and early twenties in mental health clinics and hospitals. His ADHD diagnosis, at age 25, offered David a glimmer of hope-against-hope, a hope he was almost afraid to acknowledge. It provided him with the knowledge that he wasn't "bad" or a "loser" who was unable to function properly or "crazy." It meant he wasn't "losing it!"

Finally, David realized that something physical was wrong with him, a disability that he'd struggled with, in essence, all of his life. He realized that he was no longer to blame for not behaving as everyone thought he should, that his and others' anger directed at him was misdirected. Because it wasn't "him" that was the problem. Those days were over. He could now attribute his many "failures" to something outside of "himself," in the physical realm not within his control. David's hope for a better future became real for him within one hour following Ritalin treatment. He remembers feeling "calm," a feeling he'd never experienced before, a feeling he enjoys to this day. David on Ritalin was different from how he had always been before. David likens taking Ritalin to "putting on mind glasses." He says, "It's like everything's more in focus." He calls it "a different way of being."

A "different way of being" says it perfectly. As the reader will recall from the first chapter, ADHD is a disorder that can severely impair a person's ability to function as the orchestra leader of his life. With proper treatment, one's whole life can turn around so that it is indeed "a different way of being."

David's New Concept of Control: Self-Regulation

Prior to his diagnosis, David talked incessantly, with erratic thoughts always racing through his mind, never really considering that "control" could be possible. Control as a concept appeared to have no meaning for him. Then, after his doctor prescribed Ritalin, David realized that he could exercise control. He defined control as "having power over something." In other words, "I have some power over my life (and) I have more awareness now of how much control I have." Becoming aware of his ability to exercise control provided David with a new tool he easily began to wield. A typical example of David's attitude, based on his ability to control some features of his environment, occurred when he encountered problems in everyday life. With a temporary job nearing completion, David faced the job-hunting task with, "This is one of the better cruddy situations." He analyzes a typical problem such as this, changes what he can, and accepts what he can't. He views the "bright side" as the side he has the ability to change. David manages to look at the best of whatever life has to offer him.

David is better able to control his memory. One of the first things his mother noticed after he started Ritalin was that suddenly he wasn't forgetful. It was a tremendous difference. At work, David remembers most everything, and this is how he describes it:

You see, if I write stuff down, then I forget about it and I forget where I left the piece of paper, so I just remember stuff. I remember like when I was in Algebra back like in eighth grade, I would just space out—like totally—and now I don't do that any more. Well, I still do sometimes because some things you just can't listen to any more, but it's nowhere near as bad."

David also credits Ritalin with helping him control deep-seated anger. Although angry behaviors have disappeared, angry feelings remain. In a way, you could say that David can now "apply the brakes" to his behavior, to think it through before acting on an emotion or impulse.

"I think I have a huge anger problem. I've had it for years. It's totally under control (now). It's kind of spooky. I've got a real tight lid on it. I

don't explode because of Ritalin. I don't let it out. It's just always there. It's like not letting the monster out. I walk away from anything that's going to irritate me...just for like four seconds and it's over".

David tackles whatever tasks are necessary and is able to stay on task. Extraneous stimuli appear to be ignored as he attends to career matters, schoolwork, or to his son's questions.

David's New Ability to Plan

David's needs no longer must be immediately met to prevent him from experiencing extreme frustration and anxiety. The year prior to his diagnosis, David drove from Illinois to Connecticut without enough money for gas to make it home. Today, this is an unlikely scenario because David does not act on immediate desires but instead makes detailed plans and follows through on them. After he started taking prescription Ritalin, he told his mother that he needed to plan "a reasonable course of action (for his future)." This was new terminology for David, a new way of thinking, as not much in his past appeared to have been reasonably planned. Now he has a career plan, a family plan, and important personal and interpersonal goals—and he's kept himself on target.

A New Way of Connecting for David

Prior to David's treatment, he talked constantly, never appearing to listen to what others said. His father and mother reported not feeling connected to him on an emotional or intellectual level. They reached out to David but never felt they actually reached him. They couldn't relate to him, reporting that "something was out of sync" and that David "probably felt the same way." Now, two years later, his mother reports:

It continues to amaze me how completely I feel heard and understood by David. We have a new beautiful relationship, and it feels so natural—not stilted and uncomfortable as it did before. David has eye contact with others and with me. Before Ritalin, it was quite obvious that David went out of his way to avoid making eye contact, always looking to the rigt of left or up or down but never looking directly at you. It was obvious that it was uncomfortable for David to do then, and it feels so natural now.

David's communication problems have disappeared with others, too. Never previously able to stand still and talk face-to-face and eye-to-eye with his ex-wife's parents, for example, David could immediately do so after Ritalin. His communication skills have over the last two years improved as he has felt more confident with the communication he is doing. Compassion, intuition, understanding, and an empathic awareness of other's feelings characterize David's communication with others.

With regard to David's relationship to his son, his mother reports:

Prior to his diagnosis, David did not appear to know what to do, what to say, how to act with or react to his then 5-year-old son, Christopher. I remember Christopher's first visit with his dad after Ritalin. David talked "with" Christopher—empathically, something he had never been able to do before. I remember sitting in the living room with my husband listening to David tuck Christopher in for the night. David was explaining things and telling Christopher he loved him—quietly, sincerely, and empathically.

David appears to interact with Christopher (and everyone else) on a basic level—not the surface way he had before. It was like before (Ritalin) he didn't know how to communicate with Christopher and with Ritalin he did. He read Christopher a story (another first!) and gently tucked him in for the night. That was the beginning. Two years later, David and his son have a tender, loving relationship.

His mother sums up their experiences in this way:

David's "about-face" since his "new beginnings party" following his diagnosis and Ritalin treatment has continued to grow strong and unabated. Four years later, instead of the tragedy of ending his young life that his parents feared could occur, David has taken charge of his life. He's "on-target" with his plans for his and his family's future. He faces his responsibilities squarely now instead of turning from them. David is optimistic and excited about life with much energy and great spirit.

For his part, David offers this perspective:

A lot of things have picked up in my life over the past couple of years. People die and people get sick and everything else, but things are still moving in a healthy, positive direction. It's all interdependent. Right before I was going to take Ritalin, I wasn't going to make any decisions until I was on it. So, then after that I made good decisions evidently. I went to school, which was, you know, obviously a good decision.

This is how David explained what occurred to change the direction of his life:

I was a mess. Everybody else had this one thing that I didn't—a little guy in your head telling you what's important and everything else. The thing is I'm really smart. So, I'm already ahead of the game, right? So, then I have this thing happen, where I get one of those little guys in my head, called Ritalin, and finally I can start seeing things in another dimension. So with that a lot of positive things happened.

CONCLUSION

Of course, not all have as successful a response to treatment as David had. Yet, how many of the "Davids" in the criminal justice system could be saved with intelligent diagnosis and good treatment?

Part II

Theory of How ADHD Increases Risk of Antisocial Behavior

The crucial theory in understanding how emotional and behavioral disturbances in general develop is termed the *gene-environment interaction theory* (Hinshaw, 2003; Rutter, 2003). This theory states that genetically influenced differences in an individual interact with certain environmental characteristics to produce pathology, such as antisocial behavior. Note that antisocial behavior refers to serious violations of societal rules such as rape, robbery, physical assault, and not trivial contraventions of social norms such as bad manners.

Simply translated, this scientific jargon means that some individuals are born with vulnerability such as ADHD (which, as we shall see, is typically caused by genes) that increases the likelihood that they will engage in antisocial behavior, depending upon interactions in the environment in which they are reared.

A striking example is seen in the much lower rate of alcoholism among the Japanese people, which is a consequence of a genetically influenced difference in sensitivity to alcohol. Namely, because the Japanese are overly sensitive to the toxic effects of alcohol, they are far less likely to be disposed to drink to excess. Thus, even though individuals of Japanese ancestry might be equally immersed in an environment laden in alcohol (weekends on many college campuses; for example), they will be less likely to abuse alcohol. Many other examples are evident in the marked individual differences in response to infections and to medications (Rutter, 2003).

As applied to the realm of antisocial behavior, a stunning example of vulnerability comes from research on the relationship between child maltreatment and violent criminal offenses. Although maltreatment increases the risk of later criminality by about 50 percent, most maltreated children do not become delinquents or adult criminals (Caspi et al., 2002). Hence, it is reasonable to surmise that those who do become criminals are in some way more sensitive to maltreatment than those who do not become criminals.

That this indeed is the case has been demonstrated in a large sample (442) of male children who were studied from birth to adulthood (Caspi et al., 2002). Between the ages of 3 and 11 years, 8 percent of the children experienced severe maltreatment, 28 percent experienced probable maltreatment, and 64 percent experienced no maltreatment. The environmental factor of maltreatment in and of itself, however, was insufficient to produce criminality. What was required was a *genetic vulnerability*; in this case a lower level of a brain neurotransmitter called serotonin.

A *neurotransmitter* is a brain chemical (there are about 100 of them) that transmits messages among the brain's nerve cells. Prior research had linked a low level of serotonin to violence. In this study, those children who had a gene that produced an adequate level of serotonin were virtually invulnerable to the effects of maltreatment. Thus, astoundingly, exposure to severe maltreatment did not result in violent criminality.

On the other hand, those children who had a variant of the same gene that produced a low serotonin level were much more likely to become violent offenders if maltreated. Hence, although the children with the low-active variant of the gene accounted for only 2 percent of the sample, they accounted for 44 percent of the sample's violent convictions. Moreover, 85 percent of the children who had the low-active gene and who were severely maltreated developed some form of antisocial behavior. Lastly, none of children who had the low-active gene exhibited an increased risk for antisocial behavior if they were not maltreated. Thus, even if the child had the genetic vulnerability, it did not result in criminality unless there was exposure to a maltreating environment. Let's now apply this theory to ADHD and criminal offending.

Theory of ADHD and the Link to Criminal Offending

There is a vast scientific literature relevant to the link between ADHD and criminal offending. It examines the co-occurrence of ADHD and what the psychiatric bible of mental disorders (*Diagnostic and Statistical Manual of Mental Disorders, Version IV*) calls *conduct disorder* (CD) (Hinshaw & Lee, 2003). CD is a term, applied to individuals under the age of 18, which describes various antisocial behaviors involving, for example, aggression towards people, theft, and destruction of property and other serious violations of societal rules. When individuals are caught and convicted for engaging in behaviors such as these, they receive the legal designation of "criminal."

This literature has yielded two main points of agreement. First, when ADHD and conduct disorder co-occur, the resulting antisocial disturbance is more severe, persists longer, and has an earlier onset (Hinshaw and Lee; McCabe, Rogers, Yeh, & Hough, 2004). Second, there is no doubt that ADHD and antisocial behavior occur at a greater-than-random rate (Waschbusch, 2002). For example, in a comprehensive examination of the scientific literature on co-occurrence, Washbusch (2002) concluded that 57 percent of girls and 36 percent of boys who exhibited antisocial behavior had ADHD. (Note the intriguing finding that antisocial girls were more likely to have ADHD than antisocial boys).

Indeed, the presence of ADHD results in an 11 times greater risk for developing a conduct disorder (Barkley, 2003a). Thus, this extraordinarily high co-occurrence of antisocial behavior and ADHD (especially early onset, severe ADHD), which is almost as high in community samples as it is in clinic samples (Barkley, 2003b), clearly establishes ADHD as a very significant risk factor. Indeed, the rate of co-occurrence is so high that it can be difficult to find pure cases of CD in which ADHD is not also present (Klein et al., 1997).

The most likely explanation for this high rate of co-occurrence is as follows: ADHD increases the likelihood that oppositional-defiant behaviors will develop, which in turn increases the likelihood that the more severe antisocial behaviors characteristic of conduct disorder will develop (Nigg, Goldsmith, & Sachek, 2004). Thus, Barkley (2003b) estimates that oppositional and aggressive behaviors emerge in from 40 percent to 70 percent of elementary school age children with ADHD. Yet–and this is the critical point– the development of conduct disorder, in accordance with the gene-environment interaction theory and the maltreatment example, is largely caused by the rearing of vulnerable ADHD individuals in circumstances of family adversity and impaired parenting (Barkley, 2003a); these factors contribute to a criminogenic environment, which results in criminal behavior. In short, ADHD makes a child much more vulnerable to the influences of a criminogenic environment.

Criminogenic environment refers to all those factors in the child's psychosocial environment that have been identified as contributing to the development of antisocial behavior. Because there are libraries of literature on this topic, it is sufficient here to simply note that the major environmental domains that contribute to antisocial behavior are family, school, peers, and community/neighborhood (Hawkins, 2000). Of particular note in this enormous literature is the criminogenic role of paternal absence because of birth to an unmarried mother or divorce (Lykken, 2001).

David Lykken, who received the Award for Distinguished Applications of Psychology in 2001 from the American Psychological Association, has found that 70 percent of violent delinquents and criminals were reared without fathers. Furthermore, the correlation across the 50 U.S. states between a state's violent crime rate and the proportion of young people in that state who were reared without father is .70. This association holds even after controlling for poverty, living in central cities, and birth to teenage mothers. Perhaps most intriguing is the finding that the presence of a stepfather did not decrease the risk involved in mother only-rearing, whereas boys reared by single fathers were no more at risk for serious delinquency than those brought up by both biological parents.

In summary, ADHD in childhood significantly increases the risk for criminal offending in adolescence and young adulthood, but typically only when it co-occurs with a second disorder, called *conduct disorder.* In other words, in childhood, unless there are certain environmental variables such as parental mismanagement, abuse, neglect, or substance abuses that result in ADHD precipitating an additional disorder (CD), the risk of subsequent serious antisocial behavior is minimal. Note that David's case exemplifies this point. Primarily because of quality of the parenting he had received, his risk of engaging in serious antisocial behavior was not evident until adulthood, when the cumulative effects of his ADHD rendered his life much more dysfunctional.

ADHD and Drug Abuse: Four Factors That Can Increase the Link

Lastly, note that drug abuse might be an exception to this

interaction between ADHD and CD. Severe childhood ADHD, even in the absence of CD, may increase the likelihood of subsequent drug abuse (Fischer & Barkley, 2003). The importance of this pathway to antisocial behavior warrants a more expanded treatment.

There is a wide body of research literature that demonstrates a high prevalence of ADHD among adolescent and adult substance abusers, with rates commonly ranging from 30 to 50 percent (Richardson, cited in Imperio & Anderson, 2004; Wilens, Spencer, & Biederman, 2000; Zametkin, 2002). Four major mechanisms have been proposed to explain why ADHD increases the likelihood that adolescents and young adults will develop a substance abuse disorder (Wilens, Spencer, & Biederman, 2000).

1. Increased Antisocial Tendencies

As previously discussed, many of the features of ADHD increase the likelihood of developing antisocial tendencies. These features can result in a greater likelihood of associating with antisocial peers who accept and encourage the impulsivity and free spirit, anti-authoritarian tendencies of those with ADHD. These are the same peers who are more likely to become involved in a greater degree of dangerous, high-risk behaviors such as drug and alcohol abuse. Alcohol and drug use can then become a way for many with ADHD to cope with the frustrations of life and to temporarily feel better about themselves. They can also use it as an excuse for saying and doing what they want.

2. Developing Adolescent Brains Are Vulnerable

There is evidence that changing brain circuitry in adolescence results in a vulnerability to substance abuse. Specifically, brain changes in adolescence cause a neural imbalance such that the desire for novel experiences and the motivation to repeat them develop more rapidly than does the ability to inhibit these urges and impulses. Thus, these changes promote adolescent impulsivity and novelty seeking, thereby increasing the likelihood that they will engage in risky behaviors including experimentation with addictive drugs (Chambers, Taylor, & Potenza, 2003).

Adolescents who have this vulnerability and who also have ADHD compound their risk of engaging in drug experimentation and possible addiction because their enhanced impulsivity builds upon the brain mediated natural impulsivity of this developmental period (Tarter et al., 2003).

3. Some Addictive Substances Actually Aid Attention

Furthermore, evidence also suggests that some addictive substances can actually *increase* attention. For example, most smokers report that smoking has a calming effect and also increases attention (Zametkin, 2002). And indeed there is solid scientific evidence that nicotine can increase attention (Zametkin, 2002). This may explain why in some cases, in the authors' clinical experience, individuals actually stay out of trouble while abusing the substance! The problems arise when the individuals engage in illegal acts such as drunk driving, selling and possessing illegal drugs, burglary, theft, forgery, robbery, welfare fraud, or prostitution to pay for their habits (Richardson, cited in Imperio & Anderson, 2004). Hence, some individuals with ADHD use illegal drugs to medicate the deficits in sustained attention and selective attention.

Witness the two following accounts of how substances affected the ADHD individual's sense of clarity or control. The first involves beer and the second marijuana:

The sense of relief those beers brought was a revelation. I felt free for the first time in my life. Free of the burden of overload, in control, I suddenly could think clearly, unimpeded by the jagged thoughts and feelings that had always cluttered my mind. I knew this was now! I was in this instant of time— loving this instant of time, never wanting it to go away. Where had alcohol been all my life? Welcome, beer.

Of course, I know now that from that first glorious moment I was on my way to the drinker's hall of shame, but I wouldn't discover that until much later. At the time, all I knew was that alcohol would be a part of everything important in my life. From learning to working to socializing to sex, alcohol would enable me to be me deep down, below all the turmoil and confusion.

—Case history of a young adult male cited in Miller and Blum (1996, p. 10).

The second example of how an addictive substance can bring someone clarity comes from an interview with an adolescent male who smoked marijuana a few times a day for years and was known at school as the "Weed God."

Interviewer: What is it like when you go to school high?

Client: I can sit there and it helps me concentrate. It's like medicine.

Interviewer: How does it help you concentrate?

Client: I don't know, it just does. I can concentrate.

Interviewer: Do you have concentration problems otherwise?

Client: Yeah.

Interviewer: Can you explain those to me?

Client: Don't know, like I get distracted easily but when on weed I focus more, you know?

Interviewer: Will you tell me more about being distracted?

Client: *I* don't know. I don't, like...pay attention. I'm fidgety. I can't, like, when I don't smoke weed all I do is like shake my leg or something. I can't calm down. I use it more—I think I use it more as a medicine than I do to have fun.

Interviewer: A medicine for what do you think?

Client: It calms me down. I don't have anger or whatever.

4. Some People Are Biologically Less "Reward Sensitive"

Research has shown that some individuals may be more vulnerable to becoming drug abusers because of a biological vulnerability that makes them less responsive to the sense of reward or pleasure that most people feel from activities such as eating, social interaction, or sex (Tuma, 2004). Hence they turn to addictive drugs to increase their sense of pleasure and excitement in life. ADHD can intensify this excitement seeking. As the discussion on sustained attention in Chapter 1 noted, those with ADHD are unusually prone to feeling bored.

Finally, note that stimulant medication therapy for ADHD in children not only does not predispose them to later drug use but also may decrease by as much as 50 percent the likelihood of these children developing a substance abuse disorder in adolescence (Barkley, 2003a; Wilens, 2003; Wilens, Farone, Biederman, & Funawardene, 2003). Furthermore, most cases of stimulant abuse involve a person who was not prescribed the drug (Klein-Schwartz, & McGrath, 2003).

SUMMARY

In our case study, David's chronically dysfunctional life was on the verge of culminating in jail and/or death. Despite numerous prior intensive interventions by mental-health professionals and his parents, the situation remained hopeless. Only when David received an ADHD diagnosis and treatment was he able to start turning his life around.

- There is no doubt that ADHD results in an individual becoming more vulnerable to engaging in criminal activity when exposed to a criminogenic environment. This accounts for the previously discussed high percentages of individuals in the criminal justice system that have ADHD.
- Typically, however, ADHD in and of itself does not directly lead to antisocial behavior without an interaction with a criminogenic environment (drug abuse may be an exception to this generalization).
- Once ADHD is understood, it becomes clear that certain behaviors are not as they seem. For example, evidence suggests that some addictive substances can actually *increase* attention. This may explain why certain individuals actually stay out of trouble while abusing the substance! It may also explain why some people with ADHD abuse substances: to clear their minds (also called "self-medicating").

CHAPTER 3
Causes of ADHD

This chapter will present the basis for this statement made in the introduction: There is an overwhelming international consensus that ADHD is a real and valid developmental brain disorder.

The first section of this chapter examines the developmental, biology based causes of ADHD. Specifically, we will review the complex interplay of genes and environment as factors in ADHD, including how these variables can affect actual brain structure as well as brain chemicals, called *neurotransmitters*. Special note is made of the fact that ADHD can also be acquired through brain injury. The chapter ends with a discussion of how having ADHD-like symptoms is not the same as actual ADHD, plus some myths about what causes ADHD (hint: it's not caused by "bad parenting").

It All Starts with a Genetic "Blueprint"

Once again, the car analogy comes in handy. When a manufacturer builds a car, it starts with a blueprint, a plan that includes all of the car's specifications. What happens if that blueprint includes design errors or conflicting specifications? When that final automotive product rolls off the assembly line, it will reflect these blueprint errors. For example, there might be a malfunctioning brake and transmission system. Part of the problem is structural, but there are also glitches with the fluid supply and hydraulics that exacerbate the structural problems.

Now, think of genes as the blueprint, or plan, that dictates what a *person* looks like and how he or she will function. If a person's genetic blueprint is problematic, that person will have problematic brain structures and problematic brain chemicals, including neurotransmitters. Granted, this car-brain analogy is simplistic. Yet by comparing car structures such as the brakes and transmission to brain structures and the fluid and hydraulics that allow the brakes and transmission to work to brain chemicals (including neurotransmitters), we're hoping to simplify a complex idea.

It is hard to over-emphasize this point: An international medical consensus agrees that most cases of ADHD have a genetic causation. This genetic influence results in certain brain structures and brain neurotransmitters that differ from the brains of people who do not have ADHD. These differences result in the core deficits in behavioral inhibition and sustained attention, with the consequent myriad of ADHD symptoms (Barkley, 2003b; McGuffin, Riley, & Plomin, 2001). Chapter 1 examined these two sets of core deficits.

Debunking a Myth: Majority Don't "Outgrow" ADHD

In the past, it was thought that most children "outgrew" ADHD. We now know that to be false. In fact, the majority of cases of ADHD continue from childhood into adolescence and adulthood with at least some impairing symptoms. And these cases are heavily influenced by genes (Barkley, 2003b; Todd, 2000; Farone, 2000; McGuffin, Riley, & Plomin, 2001; Thapar, 2002.). Indeed, ADHD, along with autism, schizophrenia, and bipolar disorder, is recognized as one of the most genetically influenced of all mental disorders (Farone, 2003; Imperio & Anderson, 2004; McGuffin, Riley, & Plomin).

At the time of this writing, six different genes have been identified as possibly being involved in ADHD (Farone, 2003). These findings must be considered tentative (Fisher et al., 2002), yet that does not make them less worthy of consideration. This same tentativeness also extends to other disorders that are overwhelmingly acknowledged by the scientific community as genetically caused, such as schizophrenia and manic depression (Watson, 2003). Hence, this does not mean that scientific doubt exists that genetic factors play the greatest role in causing ADHD (Barkley, 2003a); it simply means that despite huge advances in the genetics of psychological disorders, there are miles to go in our understanding of the role genetics plays in all complex behavior disorders.

The strong genetic basis of ADHD means that between 10 and 35 percent of immediate family members of children with ADHD are also likely to have the disorder, with the risk to siblings being about 32 percent (Barkley, 2003b). Even more striking is the finding that among parents who have ADHD, an estimated 57 percent of their children will also have ADHD. This finding helps to explain the fact that approximately 20 percent of children who are adopted have ADHD (Hinshaw, 2003). Namely, individuals with ADHD are more likely to be sexually impulsive and hence more likely to conceive children whom they place for adoption.

ADHD Brain Regions Show Distinct Physical Differences

Numerous studies using various scientific methods have linked the core deficits in ADHD to several specific brain regions (Newcorn, 2003). The regions commonly cited are the frontal lobes and their connections to the basal ganglia and their relationships to the cerebellum (Barkley, 2003b; Castellanos et al; 2003; Ernest et al., 2003; Pliszka, 2002). It's not important for you to remember these three areas of the brain. What's important is to understand that, in general, these brain structures, compared to the brains of those without ADHD, show the following differences:

- **Decreased activity (that is, they are under aroused)**
- **Smaller in size or having structural abnormalities**

The specifics of the brain regions and their complex connections require a solid knowledge of brain anatomy and reach beyond the scope of this book. For now, it is sufficient to regard this information as another piece of irrefutable data showing that ADHD is a *real and valid disorder.* Just as science does with medical disorders, science has linked ADHD symptoms with dysfunctional biological structures. In short, a dysfunctional brain region(s) translates into a much greater likelihood of dysfunctional behaviors.

Unfortunately, the scientific techniques used to *detect* these real brain differences cannot presently be used to reliably *diagnose* ADHD in individuals (American Academy of Pediatrics, 2001; Farone, 2003; Loo, 2003, 2004; Pliszka, 2002.).

Neurotransmitters: "Key" Brain Chemicals

As you may recall, a neurotransmitter is a brain chemical that enables the brain neurons to communicate with one another. A neuron is a nerve cell, any of the impulse-conducting cells that constitute the brain, spinal column, and nerves. We sometimes call neurotransmitters the brain's "chemical messengers" because they carry the "message"—such as a thought or action—from neuron to neuron. Proper communication between neurons allows for healthy functioning of the organism.

Now, think of a brain neuron as a lock that can be opened only by a certain kind of key. A neurotransmitter is that key. If the key is lacking or faulty, the ability to unlock the neurons will be impaired and, hence, brain functioning will be deficient. "Messages" won't be carried very effectively or efficiently. Some messages will get lost in delivery; others will go to the wrong address.

ADHD and a Neurotransmitter Called Dopamine

The current dominant theory about ADHD and neurotransmitters is this: The brains of individuals with ADHD have higher levels of a protein (Barkley, 2003b) that lowers the levels of dopamine and norepinepherine (another brain chemical, which is made from dopamine). Together, these two neurotransmitters are involved with the two primary ADHD deficits: behavioral inhibition and the regulation of attention (Castellanos, 2001; Newcorn, 2003; Swanson & Castellanos, 2002). As you'll recall from Chapter 1, deficits in inhibition ("braking") and attention result in ADHD's core symptoms and impairments.

Before continuing, we offer a reminder that little in science is simple or constant. It is the nature of science to keep pushing for clearer, better understanding. For now, however, the basic explanation above lays the foundation for understanding how neurotransmitters can affect ADHD behaviors.

Insufficient Dopamine Can Affect Selective Attention

Normally, in the brain, a certain level of random firing of nerve cells happens routinely. In a way, this routine firing allows the brain to remain "at the ready." It enables us to react more quickly when an actual stimulus presents itself, such as when we hear a loud noise and automatically duck. You could view this random firing as routine target practice. When a person's brain has a deficient level of dopamine, however, things go not routinely, but awry.

Without sufficient dopamine, *too much* random firing happens. This important finding comes from research by Dr. Nora Volkow (cited in Imperio & Anderson, 2004), an internationally recognized expert in the neurochemistry of various disorders. She found that valid signals and stimuli get lost in the internal noise. When this happens to a person, this means the person has impaired *selective attention*. In other words, the person can't distinguish important stimuli from the unimportant, the external stimuli from the internal random firing and chemical "noise." For example, jumbled all together in the person's brain are that term paper that needs finishing, the telephone ringing, the need to watch the clock to be somewhere on time, along with random neurochemical firings—all given equal importance. This can leave a person running in circles and getting nowhere fast. A person with ADHD describes the experience this way:

During any thought process, there is what I can only call a "mental storm" in my head, like fireworks. Whatever I am attempting to do is competing for attention with as many as ten other subjects, ideas and thoughts. It makes long-range planning impossible.

Insufficient Dopamine Can Also Affect Sustained Attention

Another function of dopamine is to signal the brain when something is significant and requires attention, including things that are pleasurable, novel, exciting, or exceptional. A deficient level of dopamine results in becoming easily bored, also known as having impairment in *sustained attention.*

Non-Genetic Causes of ADHD: Few and Far Between

Now that you understand, in general, the genetic causes of ADHD, we'd like to offer a few exceptions to the rule: that is, cases in which ADHD, or "ADHD-like" symptoms, is *not* caused by genetics.

Life in this modern age can produce in most of us some behaviors that resemble ADHD. We misplace our car keys. We set out on an errand, only to forget what we intended to do. We can become so overwhelmed by stress that we can't organize our thoughts. None of this means, however, that one has ADHD. It usually means, among other things, that we need to slow down.

Certain biological factors, however, can produce deficits in sustained attention and inhibition that resemble the ADHD deficits caused genetically. One must carefully distinguish between the many factors that can produce ADHD-like symptoms and the few biological factors that can cause deficits in sustained attention and inhibition similar to the deficits caused genetically.

Acquired Brain Damage

In contrast to ADHD that is caused developmentally, a small portion of individuals can develop ADHD impairments through traumatic brain injury such as a car accident (Barkley, 2003b; Brown, 2003a). In addition, prenatal exposure to alcohol or tobacco may play a role in some cases, especially for nicotine, but the research on these and other prenatal factors tends to be inconsistent and is fraught with many problems of interpretation (Linnet et al., 2003).

ADHD-Like Symptoms Do Not Equal ADHD

The factors that result in ADHD-like symptoms—but not actual ADHD—are legion. Among the most commonly cited are the following:

- **Physical and sexual abuse**
- **Post-traumatic stress disorder**
- **Pure oppositional defiant disorder and conduct disorder**
- **Misinterpretation of normal levels of over-activity and inattention in the school setting.**

The extent to which other conditions can mimic ADHD is often greatly exaggerated. Perhaps the most commonly echoed erroneous example is the notion that a vast number of normally rambunctious boys in school settings could readily be diagnosed with ADHD. Nothing could be further from the truth! To diagnose ADHD (Combined Type), the *Diagnostic and Statistical Manual, Version 4—Text Revision* (DSM IV TR) requires a minimum of six symptoms of inattention and hyperactivity that occur often. Research indicates that only from 7 to 23 percent of normal boys has any one particular DSM symptom of hyperactivity that occurs *often* (Barkley, 1998).

To be sure, the aforementioned factors and innumerable others can result in *some* ADHD symptoms. Such factors can also *increase or decrease the impairments* associated with ADHD. Yet a few swallows do not a summer make. In other words, having a few symptoms is not the same as having the disorder called ADHD.

For example, at the time of this writing, excessive television viewing is the current "flavor of the month" and has been wrongly implicated in the media as a possible cause of ADHD. The actual study, on which many of these erroneous new stories are based, however, is far more cautious (Christakis, Zimmerman, DiGiuseppe, & McCarty, 2004). In fact, the researchers explicitly state that their findings regarding *attention problems* cannot be automatically construed as applying to ADHD. In other words, attention problems and ADHD are not the same thing. Furthermore, and most importantly, it states that *"we cannot draw causal inferences from these associations"* (p. 711).

Controversial Potential (But So Far Not Likely) Causes
The scientific status of developmental or acquired brain impairment as being major causes of ADHD is secure. The same cannot be said of the innumerable other so-called biological causes ("flavors of the month") that appear and disappear with considerable frequency. Among those most commonly cited are:
- Food additives
- Thyroid condition
- Sugar
- Allergies
- Mineral deficiencies
- Environmental toxins (lead)
- Candida yeast.

These alleged causes have undergone comprehensive critical review (Arnold, 2002), and here is the verdict: the scientific evidence validating these causes was nonexistent or, at best, promising. The term *promising* is a siren adjective that means that the theory is not dead in the water but requires much more evidence before it can be accepted as proven.

That said, a few possible exceptions might prove the aforementioned rule. For example, especially in preschoolers, diet and allergy may be a factor in a small percentage of cases (Center for Science in the Public Interest, 1999).

Lastly, note that various psycho-social factors such as poor parenting can worsen the impaired functioning subsequent to having ADHD or contribute to the development of a comorbid disorder such as conduct disorder, but these psycho-social factors do not *cause* the disorder (Barkley, 2003b).

The Final Word: Accurate Diagnosis Is Critical

ADHD is a chronic disorder caused by brain dysfunction that results in a configuration of symptoms that create various and significant life impairments. To be accurately diagnosed with ADHD, a person must undergo a careful evaluation conducted by an expert specifically trained in this type of diagnosis. Accurate diagnosis is critical if we are to avoid overdiagnosis or misdiagnosis.

As with all biologically caused disorders, certain conditions may mimic the disorder (the medical term is *phenocopies*) but are not the real disorder. For example, symptoms of *chest pain and dizziness* may herald a heart attack or something else entirely unrelated to a heart attack. What is required is expert diagnosis. We'll explore this topic further when we discuss diagnosis. For now, suffice it to say: A lousy diagnosis means a lousy professional, not a lousy disorder.

SUMMARY

- ADHD is primarily caused by inheriting a strong genetic predisposition that results in certain brain regions being smaller and less active—when compared to the brains of people without ADHD—as well as abnormalities in certain brain chemicals.

- This genetic disorder, which individuals are born with, then interacts with various environmental risk factors, resulting in greater or lesser degrees of impairment in functioning.

- Complex scientific theories aside, this much is known: ADHD has a strong genetic component, and neurotransmitters are involved. The irrefutable proof of this is that stimulant medications operate on neurotransmitters and show great success in the treatment of ADHD.

- Having "ADHD-like symptoms" is not the same as having ADHD. Diagnosis of ADHD (Combined Type) requires a minimum of six specific symptoms of inattention and hyperactivity that occur often.

- Poor parenting does not cause ADHD, but it can worsen impaired functioning in a child who has ADHD.
- The exception to genetically caused ADHD is ADHD deficits caused by brain injury.

CHAPTER 4
The Initial Law Enforcement Contact

The average person's first and perhaps only contact with the criminal justice system happens when a police officer stops him or her for a traffic violation. Of course, citizens also seek the police when they've been the victims of a crime or when they're lost and needing directions. Others experience "first contact" by being a witness or a suspect in a criminal investigation. In general, however, traffic stops account for the most common interactions between police officers and civilians. Most stops proceed routinely. For many people with undiagnosed and untreated ADHD, however, that interaction can be fraught with potential for making huge errors of judgment, with serious repercussions.

Even under the best of circumstances, a traffic stop can prove stressful for all concerned, including the police officer. Adding undiagnosed ADHD to the equation can magnify existing stresses and create all sorts of new ones. Recall for a moment what you've learned about the nature and disabilities inherent in ADHD. Remember some of the behavior buzzwords, such as:

- Impulsivity
- Irritability
- Restlessness
- Defiance of authority
- Inability to prioritize what's important
- Trouble paying attention

It's easy to see how some persons with ADHD might have a more-problematic-than-average first contact with the police.

For starters, many people with ADHD tend to make even minor situations worse through poor decision-making under duress.

In this chapter, we review the routine traffic stop from two points of view: the police officer's and the motorist's. The reader will learn how, at various times in the process, the motorist's untreated ADHD behavior and the officer's misinterpreting of the behavior can negatively affect final outcome. Building on this understanding, this chapter explains how to recognize ADHD symptoms in various criminal behaviors, including gang activity. This information can help the officer suppress a potentially escalating situation in the field, learn ways to identify these individuals for assistance in solving crimes, and perhaps include in the record a recommendation for ADHD evaluation

A Routine Traffic Stop

During any traffic stop, a police officer must make a series of decisions quickly. The officer, a human being capable of errors and wrong assumptions, usually possesses little or no knowledge of the person being stopped, including what kind of day he is having, what mood he might be in, or problems that weigh on his mind. At the same time, once the officer elects to make a stop, he follows a standard action protocol that is probably unknown to the average citizen and, as a result, could be easily misunderstood. How well the interaction proceeds depends largely on smooth, predictable behavior from both sides.

Let's look at a "normal" traffic stop from the perspective of both the officer and the motorist. The motorist might have noticed that a squad car slowed, turned around, and is now following him. He may observe the squad car leave a place where it had been parked and begin following him. At this point, the motorist's lifestyle and past encounters with police will influence the level of anxiety he'll experience—from very little to a great deal—as well as any preconceived notions surrounding what could happen at a potential traffic stop.

If the motorist has been involved in other law-breaking

behaviors recently, his emotions and guilt can escalate far beyond what the officer, meanwhile, might be expecting from a standard traffic violation. Suppose he possesses illegal drugs, is underage, has alcohol in his car, or had broken into a house two days ago. No doubt he would be experiencing a state of anxiety higher than average. On the other hand, if he has done nothing wrong, in his opinion, his anxiety at potentially being stopped might be very low. More benign thoughts might run through this motorist's mind as well. Perhaps he was driving only a few miles over the limit and is hoping to get by with just a warning.

Like most of us in this situation, a motorist might ask himself in rapid and sometimes jumbled order some of the following questions.

- Why am I being followed?
- Just how fast was I going?
- If I am stopped, will I get a ticket?
- How many tickets have I already gotten in the past year?
- Is my driver's license suspended or revoked? Has it expired?
- Have I been drinking?
- Have I had too much to drink?
- Have I been using illegal drugs?
- Do I have illegal drugs or alcohol with me now and am I underage?
- Have I committed another crime recently?
- Do I have an outstanding warrant for my arrest?

While he is reviewing these questions in his mind, time seems to have eerily slowed. Meanwhile, the officer is making mental notes about the motorist's vehicle and assessing the situation carefully, as trained. He may be notifying dispatch that he is about to make a traffic stop. The officer has given dispatch the description of the vehicle, license plate number, and location of the possible stop. The dispatcher has begun entering this information into a computer with national links to determine if the vehicle is stolen or the registered owner is wanted for other crimes. The officer following the motorist's car is probably looking for a safe place to make the traffic stop, away from dangerous traffic patterns or dark secluded areas. It may mean several miles and many minutes of waiting for the motorist, which might add to his anxiety, especially if he doesn't understand the reason for the delay. During this time, even an innocent person may have remembered all sorts of past misdeeds and created considerable stress for himself. Yet the average person is able to remain relatively calm and collected.

Contrast: A Traffic Stop with a Motorist Who Has ADHD

Now, consider a motorist named Chris. He has ADHD, but he doesn't know it. Neither does the police officer who is about to stop Chris's car. In short, what happens next is anybody's guess. If ADHD behavior problems have been severe in the past for Chris, here are new variables he brings to the "routine" traffic stop:

- Chris might have a record of speeding, reckless driving, driving under suspension, or driving under the influence of alcohol or drugs.
- He might have tried to elude police in the past and be thinking about trying it again now.
- He might be angry at himself for once again "messing up" and getting another traffic ticket.
- He might have had previous problems with authority—parents, teachers, other police officers, you name it.

All these factors churn in Chris's mind when the officer flicks on the top lights in his patrol car and perhaps activates the siren. The anxiety levels for both Chris and the officer ratchet upward. The officer, knowing this is one of the most dangerous situations that officers routinely face, focuses his awareness of all activity occurring in Chris's vehicle. The officer is preparing to react quickly—and with very little information—in dealing with Chris and any other vehicle occupants; he must be prepared for either a routine event or a worst-case-scenario where everything goes sour.

What happens next largely depends on the mood of both the officer and Chris, not to mention Chris's sobriety level, his mental state, and the attitude of all persons involved in the stop. When Chris pulls his car over, after being directed to stop, the officer, as trained, approaches the car cautiously and remains observant of the car's occupants—those already visible and those who might be out of view. It's nighttime, so the officer shines a bright spotlight into the rear-view mirror of Chris's car. This action serves to both illuminate the car's interior (making any hidden occupants more visible) and make it difficult for the driver to observe the one or two officers approaching the car, thus increasing the officer's safety.

Chris doesn't know all this. To him, it just feels like an authority figure being aggressive. His anxiety level shot through the roof a few minutes ago, taking his self-control with it, and he just *reacts*. Without thinking, he exits the car, starts pacing in an agitated way, and impulsively blurts out in a rude tone of voice to the officer, "Why did you stop me and what's up with the spotlight in my mirror?"

Caught Up in Impulsive Behavior

Caught up in his impulsivity and hyperactivity, Chris has just made two huge mistakes, both of which could escalate a simple traffic warning memo into a summons—or worse—not to mention making it look like he's surely guilty of more than running that stop sign. Chris isn't thinking about consequences. And he's certainly forgotten what his parents always advised him: If you're ever stopped by the police, stay in the car, turn the dome light on at night, keep your hands on the top of the steering wheel, and remain seated for the entire time.

Faced with such apparent hostility, a well-trained officer will immediately go on alert. This is human nature. If Chris could stop to think about it—"put the brakes" on his behavior—he might realize he's made a tense situation worse and start doing damage control. What's more, officers *do not* like it when motorists leave the car; they are trained that it could be an aggressive act. (It might not be, but officers can't read minds anymore than average citizens can; they are trained to hope for the best but expect the worst.) When a motorist exits his car, officers might suspect he is hiding something in his vehicle or is trying to distract the officer's attention while another person in the car is doing something else.

Normally, the officer is trained to try to calm the situation by speaking softly yet firmly as he makes the required requests for driver's license and car registration information. If Chris continues to act aggressively or even inappropriately defensive, the situation can slide downhill quickly. If fears are calmed on both sides, the situation may de-escalate almost as quickly as it had escalated. Even body language can play a role here, as many with ADHD are not aware of their facial expressions and jerky hand gestures.

If Motorists Act Suspiciously, Maybe They Are Guilty

From an experienced law-enforcement officer's perspective, the more agitated and defensive the motorist becomes, the more scrutiny and suspicion that person attracts. Instinct and training bear out that the potential is there to discover a more serious law-breaking behavior. This is not always true, but the increased scrutiny may still result in the detection of illegal alcohol, drugs, weapons, or other criminal activity that might have gone undetected if the motorist had displayed a calmer demeanor.

Based on co-author Patrick Hurley's law enforcement experience, duties as a probation officer, and his review of past criminal and traffic records of persons with diagnosed ADHD, it appears that they have more frequent contacts with law enforcement officers and experience a seemingly greater degree of negative outcomes from those contacts. In other words, they have more tickets, more arrests for criminal activity, and a higher frequency of having their driving privileges suspended, revoked, or barred. The odds are higher than average of having an ongoing relationship with the upper levels of the criminal justice system such as the courts, probation, prison, and parole.

All police officers seem to develop a sense for identifying what you could call the "weak link" in a group of suspects. Based on co-author Hurley's experience, persons with ADHD fit in this category. With a newfound understanding of ADHD, Hurley began recalling individuals from years ago that he might now suspect as having ADHD usually were very easy to spot or pick out from a group of people by both their verbal and their body language. For example, the person tends to fidget and not make eye contact. This might look as though the person is lying or nervous, when in fact this might be his normal demeanor. And people with ADHD often are very bad liars.

Identifying ADHD Traits in Criminal Activity

The following traits appear to be common among persons with ADHD who are suspected of criminal activity:

- They often create elaborate and unconvincing scenarios for what has occurred.
- They have difficulty keeping their story straight.
- They have trouble keeping secrets.
- They are not good at lying, and their faces may flush or betray a guilty look almost immediately upon questioning.

Any experienced law enforcement officer will know how to interpret these traits. In fact, a person with such traits proves a valuable tool to the officer. Because suspects in a case are normally separated to preclude collaboration of stories, the potential suspect displaying ADHD traits is probably the first one the officer will question. Typically, his story is hopelessly filled with holes and contradictions absent in the others' stories. Questions that draw complicated answers may bring more questions from the officer.

ADHD Self-Sabotage: Bragging About Crimes

In the author's experience, many criminals who seem to self-sabotage probably had ADHD. They are the ones who brag to all their friends—and even some of their casual acquaintances—about their involvement in criminal behavior, never stopping to think that those persons might tell others or alert authorities.

You probably have read of persons breaking into houses and stealing items such as video cameras and then filming their criminal activity to show others. They often have the videotape in the car when officers stop them, or it is common knowledge because so many people have seen the video that the person considers a "trophy" of his criminal exploits.

Most police officers can tell stories of persons who have done something to sabotage themselves. The author had more than one case where someone lost his wallet behind at the scene of the crime or drove down the road knocking down rural mailboxes and, unknowingly ripped off the license plate of the vehicle, making it easy for officers to apprehend him.

Some of this type of spontaneous and impulsive behavior relates to our earlier discussions on self-esteem and gaining acceptance of others. Some persons with untreated ADHD may think their peers will admire them or accept them if they do outrageous stunts. Some more dominant predatory criminals may use the person to do some of their dirty work for them. The criminal with ADHD often wants to please those he views as better criminals and is happy to comply.

Some of these more skilled criminals also recognize the potential risks of being too closely aligned with the ADHD-type criminal and use layers of protection to employ these people in criminal activity. This especially is evident in gang activity.

The Gang Connection

We could speculate that a classic gang "wannabe" might have a greater chance of having ADHD, and here are a few reasons why:

- **The gang provides him with an acceptance (even though it may be a false acceptance) that he lacks** from family and other friends.

- These "wannabes" are eager to show others that they will do anything necessary.
- They want to be able to tell their friends and acquaintances how valuable they are to the gang, especially if they are failing in other areas of their life.
- They will usually embellish their stories and accomplishments to outsiders to seem even more dangerous and tough than they actually are.
- They are willing to accept this fear that their friends may have of them as a substitute for actual friendship.

To the police, these "wannabes" often stand out as not quite fitting the image of the stereotypical gang member. They are potentially good "snitches" for the police because their need for acceptance and importance is met by either the gang members or the police who deal with them. In the author's experience, the more their stature decreases in the gang, the more likely they are to become informants for the police. They seek acceptance at all costs. Unfortunately, some officers may use these people for information with little or no concern for what might happen to them later on from their fellow gang members.

A professional officer who recognizes a person like this should also take necessary steps to help protect this person from the dangerous consequences of providing information to law enforcement. Many of these individuals are very likeable. Most experienced police officers know of people like this. The role that Joe Pesci played in the "Lethal Weapon" films would be a good example of this type of person. As Leo Goetz, Pesci displays classical ADHD symptoms in those movies—wanting to be accepted but instead being picked on and made fun of by the Mel Gibson and Danny Glover characters and at the same time showing a genuine need to be friends with the police and having a soft, sentimental side that he doesn't like sharing.

What Can Law Enforcement Do?

The street cop or investigator can mention traits in an investigation report that a psychologist, defense attorney, or probation/parole officer could later use. It is probably not a good idea for a street cop to tell someone he needs to be evaluated for ADHD. Yet, by recognizing ADHD signs in these individuals, the officer may help suppress a potentially escalating situation in the field. Officers can obviously learn some ways to identify these individuals to help solve crimes. And, an officer might become close enough to an individual to suggest that the person could be helped professionally.

SUMMARY

The average person's first and most frequent contact with the criminal justice system happens with a routine traffic stop. When the motorist has untreated ADHD, variables enter the equations that raise the likelihood of a problematic encounter. These variables include common ADHD deficits such as impulsiveness, irritability, restlessness, defiance of authority, inability to prioritize what's important, and trouble paying attention. By knowing how to interpret these behaviors, a traffic officer can prevent a tense situation from escalating.

When attempting to identify individuals with ADHD among criminal suspects, pay attention to those who create elaborate and poorly convincing scenarios for what has occurred, who have trouble keeping their story straight and keeping secrets, who are not good at lying, and whose faces may flush or betray a guilty look almost immediately upon questioning.

An individual with ADHD may be particularly vulnerable to being a "gang wannabe." A professional officer who recognizes a person like this should take necessary steps to help protect this person from the dangerous consequences of providing information to law enforcement.

The street cop or investigator can mention possible ADHD traits in an investigation report that could prove useful to the psychologist, defense attorney, or probation/parole officer.

CHAPTER 5
Court and Judgment

Chapter 4 explored the ways in which common ADHD deficits of attention, hyperactivity, impulsivity, and irritability leave some individuals with untreated ADHD more vulnerable to meeting arrest. From this point on in the criminal justice system, those same deficits continue making a bad situation worse for the offender. Once in jail, for example, the offender might become combative and find himself in restraints or, conversely, display great emotional upset, crying as he realizes he has once again "messed up" and disappointed his family. Moaning that his life is over could force jail staff to place him on suicide watch. As bad as this can be for the defendant with untreated ADHD, it's about to get worse.

At any point along the way, knowledge about ADHD among criminal justice professionals could mean all the difference. This chapter discusses ways in which four critical groups of professionals—the pre-trial release staff, prosecutors, defense attorneys, and judges may seek to distinguish a defendant who possibly has ADHD and thus attempt to include some kind of assessment or follow-up treatment as part of the sentencing.

It is important to remember: Some defendants with ADHD land in the criminal justice system largely because of their significant brain impairments. These impairments do not suddenly vanish once they are arrested. Instead, the stress stemming from the arrest usually only exacerbates their ADHD symptoms

Pre-Trial Interviews and Defendants with ADHD
The first stage for most prisoners in the court system today

is being interviewed by a pre-trial release staff member, which typically occurs the day after the arrest. These staff members are often employees of the local department of community corrections or the courts. Their interviews aim to establish how persons charged with crimes should be released from jail, in one of three following ways:

- **Release on their own recognizance (the most frequent outcome)**
- **Release with supervision to the department of corrections**
- **Held in jail on bond.**

The interviewer checks background information such as residential and employment stability, family or other ties to the community, financial status, and past criminal conduct and evaluates the prisoner's cooperation with the interviewer. Then the interviewer provides this information to the judge conducting the initial court appearance. Judges may follow the recommendation of the interviewer or make their own decisions.

At this crucial step in the criminal justice system, past criminal contacts and cooperation with the pre-trial interviewers may pose the biggest problems for prisoners with ADHD. An individual might have a series of past arrests, often multiple arrests within the last few months. Perhaps a particular crisis—such as a job loss or domestic assault following a relationship breakup—has prompted this string of bad behavior. Perhaps the crisis follows a poorly planned impulsive act, such as a burglary or theft. It could be complicated by drug or alcohol abuse, a frequent problem that some experts view as an attempt to self-medicate or to numb the painful and self-defeating internal cognition "I am bad and will never amount to anything."

At any rate, the defendant finds himself in jail, with his history often reflecting one or more of the following characteristics:

- **Numerous job changes, usually from one low-paying job to another.**

- A tendency to move frequently.
- Alienation from parents, relatives, roommates, or significant others who for most people form a support network.
- Weak ties to the community, even if he has have lived there all his life, because he has burned bridges with friends and past employers.
- Limited financial resources because of dysfunctional and poor money handling habits.
- Criminal records, or "rap sheets," full of past crimes, pending charges, failures to appear at hearings, driving under suspension/revocation, and unsuccessful probationary status.

In other words, the defendant scores very few points for being released on his own recognizance. (Note: Even though we use the masculine pronoun here, female defendants can fit the same profile.)

In addition, he has probably experienced this sequence of events before and is totally frustrated with either himself or "the system." He displays hostility, indifference, or dishonesty to the pre-trial interviewer. Often, he may have even attempted using a friend's or relative's name and birth date during booking. Such action usually results in a recommendation of bond rather than release. This further frustrates the individual who, unless he has family support intact, can find himself in jail with no one willing to provide his bail.

What Can Pre-Trial Interviewers Do?

It is important both to know the common traits of attention deficit disorder and to ask, "Have you ever been diagnosed with attention deficit hyperactivity disorder?" and "Have you ever been prescribed Ritalin?" For many, an ADHD diagnosis unfortunately carries a stigma and they are loathe to admit it. Even though the jail staff might have already asked these questions, the prisoner may respond in a different way this time and thus not "fall through the cracks."

Once offenders are brought into the judicial system, several possibilities exist. If they are lucky enough to be released, the judge will sometimes recommend the option of release with supervision. This usually requires them to stay in touch or report to a pre-trial release officer, pending the outcome of their court case. This person monitors the offender's requirements of release, which often involve seeking substance abuse evaluation and treatment, maintaining a stable residence, getting and keeping a job, obtaining an attorney or court appointment of an attorney, and making court appearances.

Judges and ADHD Defendants Before Trial

The person released is often responsible for staying in touch with the pre-trial release officer and keeping him informed of attempts to comply with the court's pre-trial release conditions. This is problematic for many ADHD defendants for the following reasons (remember the ADHD deficits regarding working memory, keeping track of time, understanding consequences, and acting impulsively):

- They have a history of trouble keeping track of appointments, meaning they're more likely to miss follow-up hearings and other important events.
- They tend to change residence without giving notice, neglecting to stay in touch with the pre-trial release officer and even their own attorneys.
- They procrastinate on the other conditions of release, such as seeking substance abuse treatment or counseling.
- They often violate no-contact orders or other court restrictions associated with their release.
- They frequently fail to appear at subsequent court hearings such as arraignments, or preliminary hearings, which can result in a warrant of arrest and revocation of their pre-trial release.

- They find themselves back in jail with a bond required for their release.
- Even if they are initially released on their own recognizance, defendants with ADHD might procrastinate on retaining an attorney or filling out an application for a court-appointed attorney.

Of course, all of this only leads to more frustration for the individual and the attorney. This also can lead to the courts, prosecutors, and even their own attorney viewing such defendants as indifferent to the pending criminal charges against them.

Some defense attorneys will often withdraw from such defendants' cases because the clients seem unconcerned about assisting in their own defense, as evidenced by failures to make appointments with the attorney or follow his or her advice. The defendants with ADHD will often show up an hour or day early or an hour or day late for hearings. They may have even met with their attorney the day before yet still forget their hearing the following day. They often show up unprepared, without an attorney, or ask for postponement so they can get an attorney they should have gotten weeks or months earlier.

Although the aforementioned behavior could be intentional manipulation by some individuals, most people involved with the courts will tell you that quite a few defendants seem intelligent and well meaning yet chronically have trouble coping with the requirements of "the system." The courts, however, are based on structure and compliance, so naturally this conflicts with defendants' cognitive problems in these very same areas.

This phenomenon tries the patience of the prosecutors, judges, bailiffs, and their own attorneys. It increases the likelihood that their court hearings will have more negative outcomes than those of defendants who are more compliant. The offenders with untreated ADHD are more likely to impatiently advise their attorneys to just get the process over with so they can be done with it. This is the classic tendency of dealing with the moment's problems without concern for what might lay ahead for them, such as jail, or suspended jail sentences, probation, compliance with probation, violation of probation hearings, and more sanctions or even revocation of probation and more negative outcomes.

These individuals often clog up the court system, and criminal justice system professionals find them terribly difficult and frustrating to deal with.

What Can Judges Do Pre-Trial?

By knowing and recognizing the traits of ADHD and encouraging jail and pre-trial release staff to screen for signs of these characteristics, judges could make a condition of release that the defendant pursue an evaluation or, if previously diagnosed, resume counseling and doctors' recommendations.

Prosecutors and ADHD Defendants

A prosecutor typically views ADHD defendants in a number of ways. Primarily, they are often inept criminals and the prosecutor's cases against them are usually very strong, frequently the "open and shut case." Clear and convincing evidence with corroboration usually exists, including the defendant's confession of guilt or an easily discounted, unbelievable scenario of what occurred. Often, they are co-defendants with other ADHD individuals who are equally impulsive. The police will separate the two or three individuals and quickly discover widely different accounts of their actions. This often leads to one or more of the individuals coming clean or making a plea bargain in an attempt to get a better deal for themselves.

Other common characteristics of the ADHD defendant include, as mentioned earlier, missed court hearings and frustrated defense attorneys because the defendant systematically removes potential bargaining chips the attorney could normally use. The defendant may have multiple pending charges that give the prosecutor the upper hand in any plea-bargaining situations.

ADHD defendants often turn up in both misdemeanor and felony courts. They are usually well known to the police, the prosecutors, and the judges. Their repeated court appearances and seeming lack of motivation to change their behavior tend to cause poor outcomes for these individuals in the legal system.

If given probation, they find themselves back in court for contempt of court or revocation hearings for both technical and law-breaking violations of probation. Rarely do these hearings go favorably for the defendant.

What Can Prosecutors Do?

By knowing the traits of ADHD and encouraging the police, jails, pre-trial release, defense attorneys, and the courts to do the same, prosecutors can assist the defendant in being more effective with his defense and hopefully reduce both missed court appearances and recidivism, both of which waste prosecutors' time and the public's tax dollars.

Defense Attorneys and ADHD Defendants

Defendants with ADHD are a defense attorney's nightmare for several reasons, including the following most common:

- They have a tendency to sabotage most efforts the defense attorney makes to help them.
- They don't follow suggestions or take directions on recommendations.
- They frequently want to misdirect blame to others, minimize their own behavior, and systematically dismantle potential bargaining tools.
- They may change residence without notifying the courts or even their attorneys.
- They miss appointments with their attorneys and important court hearings.
- They are more likely to violate no-contact orders and pre-trial release conditions or neglect or refuse to follow directives to obtain evaluations or substance abuse treatment. This greatly enhances the prosecution's case and provides more ammunition to use against the defendant.

- They may fire their attorney for not doing what they want the attorney to do.
- They often force their attorney into progressively weaker positions so that, ultimately, the defense attorney can do little else but seek the best possible plea-bargain agreement available.

Defendants with untreated ADHD can sabotage a best outcome in other ways, too. For example, consider the following scenario:

The defense attorney explains the possible negative ramifications and probably feels in the back of his mind that the defendant is very likely to fail at intermediate sanctions that they might be seeking such as probation. The attorney is obligated to get the best possible deal, even if it means a longer suspended jail sentence and fewer immediate consequences. The defendant, however, sees only the "bottom line" of probation versus jail time and jumps at the chance for probation, not fully understanding that he may be setting himself up for a prolonged and difficult ordeal in terms of compliance.

What Can Defense Attorneys Do?

By knowing and recognizing ADHD traits in defendants, the defense attorney can identify and troubleshoot potential problems in the attorney-client relationship, especially those relating to keeping appointments with the attorney, making court appearances in a timely fashion, and assisting with their own defense. This might involve making it abundantly clear—in precise, concrete terms—the importance of staying in touch or checking in daily. It might also involve taking pains to explain very simply the choices available and the repercussions of each. Attorneys can also recommend assessment for those who may need diagnosis for ADHD or counseling and following the doctor's orders regarding medication for those who were previously diagnosed.

Pre-Sentence Investigators and ADHD Defendants

After a plea bargain or plea or finding of guilt, often a month or so elapses while a court-ordered pre-sentence investigation is conducted into the defendant's background. Typically, pre-sentence investigators work for local community-based correctional service agencies.

The investigator's job is to extensively investigate the defendant's past criminal record, socio-economic upbringing, educational records, history of alcohol or drug treatment, family situation, job performance, and stability, as well as obtain a statement from the victim on the crime's impact. Investigators also seek to establish the amount of restitution that should be ordered and will usually include an opportunity for defendants to state their idea of a fair disposition to the case.

Based on all these factors, the investigator issues a recommendation to the court regarding suitable outcome in the best interest of the community. This recommendation also takes into account local jail populations, availability of community-based halfway houses, prison populations, and current numbers of persons on probation or parole. The recommendation is not binding to the judge or the prosecutor, although both tend to follow it. The defense attorney usually argues for a lesser sentence than is recommended by the pre-sentence investigator.

An investigator looking at a defendant with untreated ADHD will often find the following information:

- A long history of past criminal offenses involving crimes of an impulsive nature and involvement in abuse of alcohol and drugs.
- A poor traffic motor vehicle record, including speeding, reckless driving, and multiple accidents. This is usually followed by driver's license suspensions or revocations and subsequent charges of driving under suspension or revocation.
- A family history that may include being adopted, coming from a dysfunctional family whose other family members are well known to the criminal justice system, or, just as commonly, coming from seemingly good families with no other past

involvement in the criminal justice system and who consider the defendant the family's "black sheep."
- Substance abuse and temper-related problems such as assaults.
- An educational background indicating long-term problems in school or academic underperformance.

Dropping out of school early is common, with the defendant usually claiming boredom or problems with authority figures, such as teachers and principals. Suspensions or expulsion from school may appear. Often the defendant may have succeeded in elementary and high school, only to suddenly drop out for surprising reasons. Or he goes to college and his academic performance plunges as the stimulus of newfound freedom and independence allows him to do as he pleases. Many of these defendants express a desire to return to school or obtain their G.E.D. Many indicate they want to pursue advanced degrees that vastly contradict the person's previous academic performance. For example, they might say they want to go to medical school when they are high-school dropouts.

Defendants with ADHD frequently appear to be highly intelligent or gifted in a particular area such as computers, art, or acting. They may struggle with traditional teaching methods, however, and the structure that schools impose.

Due to the paradoxical nature of ADHD, many persons will not fit the normal model for hyperactivity and in fact may have excellent academic records due to the often obsessive and "hyperfocusing" nature of the disorder plus a desire to prove to themselves or others that the struggles in their minds are controllable. They may have been successful in structuring and controlling how they conduct their lives, which sometimes masks the underlying sense of underachievement they harbor. To the outsider, it may seem ridiculous that this person views himself as a failure because he seems to be doing so well in many respects. In fact, many people totally discount the idea that the person may have ADHD because he seems to possess intelligence and good looks, be socially outgoing, and have "everything going for him." People are shocked that this person may have run afoul of the law or have a drinking or drug abuse problem.

What Can Pre-Sentence Investigators Do?

By knowing the traits of ADHD and asking the right questions during the interview, the investigator might hold out the last hope for the defendant with ADHD. He or she could provide the "safety net" that prevents this defendant from slipping through the cracks. Investigators commonly discover an earlier diagnosis of ADHD or prescription for Ritalin or other stimulant medication. If there are indications of ADHD, they might recommend that the defendant be assessed immediately before sentencing to make a determination. During the sentencing assessment, the investigator—although not minimizing the defendant's involvement in criminal conduct—may be able to use the information gathered as a "possible" mitigating factor in determining appropriate action the court may wish to take.

By sentencing time, the ADHD client's previous actions have often placed him at a great disadvantage. Past criminal records, lack of compliance, or lack of success with pre-trial and post-trial requirements bear heavily on the outcome. Some people might never even have made it to the department of corrections to complete their pre-sentence investigation interview.

The pre-sentence investigation may show a defendant whose past is riddled with failed opportunities to comply with society's structure. The defendant's noncompliance with previous restrictions such as driving under suspension, failures to appear, and probation or parole violations all come back to haunt him or her.

The pre-sentence investigation will no doubt expose all these past missed opportunities. The recommendation will no doubt be for more stringent sanctions. The prosecutor has a strong case to ask for and receive a stricter sentence. The defense may be put in the position to just minimize the damage and get what it can for the client.

Sentencing Judges and ADHD Defendants

At sentencing, the defendant with ADHD commonly will attempt to tell the court that he knows he has failed in the past but is ready now to comply fully if just given this one more opportunity. The defendant may actually believe this to be true. Family or friends may be called to testify and often are not only ineffective but also actually damaging to the defendant's cause.

A sentence with a number of days or months in jail, or years in prison may be imposed. A portion of or the entire sentence may be suspended and the defendant placed on probation. As a repeat offender, the defendant may be sentenced to prison or jail time without probation.

Defendants with ADHD often receive probation, but are frequently doomed to failure from the onset. Sometimes they might be better off to do their jail time if the crime is a lesser one.

What Can Sentencing Judges Do?

By knowing the traits of ADHD, the judge can better assess the proper sentence to impose. Creative or alternative sentencing may be attempted. As a condition of either probation or incarceration, the judge may order evaluation, ongoing counseling, group support attendance, and the like.

SUMMARY

- Some offenders with untreated ADHD enter the criminal justice system because of brain deficits. Once a person with untreated ADHD enters this system, those deficits often conspire to create progressively worse outcomes.
- ADHD savvy criminal justice professionals including the pre-trial release staff, prosecutors, defense attorneys, and judges—can learn to distinguish a defendant who might have untreated ADHD and

attempt to include some kind of assessment or follow-up treatment as part of the sentencing.

SPINNING OUT OF CONTROL

CHAPTER 6
Probation and Prison

Chapter 5 explored how, prior to the defendant's sentencing, criminal justice professionals can identify defendants who might have ADHD and recommend screening. This chapter looks at the post-sentencing opportunities for probation officers or jail/prison staff to determine if an ADHD screening might be in order for probationers and inmates. The very same ADHD deficits that led to the defendant being arrested in the first place—and then poorly navigating the criminal justice system, resulting in a guilty plea or verdict—can also pose problems for the person with ADHD and for probation officers and prison personnel.

How ADHD Deficits Can Affect Probation

Probation provides an alternative to jail for defendants found guilty or who plead guilty to crimes. Probation basically works like this: The court receives a guilty plea or verdict, and sentencing can follow immediately on minor cases or be delayed for weeks or months on more serious offenses that require a pre-sentence investigation.

Typically, a judge imposes a county jail term (180 days, for example) or a prison term (five years, for example). Lesser offenses bring county jail terms; more serious matters result in prison time. Jail often serves more as a holding facility rather than a correctional facility, seldom offering the range of services available to prisoners at state penal institutions. Sometimes jail inmates can work during the day and return to jail at night.

The judge often imposes the sentence and then suspends all or part of it, leaving the remaining time hanging over the defendant's head during a probationary period. For example, a 180-day jail sentence might have the defendant serve 10 days in jail and suspend the 170 remaining days while placing the defendant on probation for from one to three years. Typically, judges impose additional conditions such as performing public community service work and or completing school, undergoing counseling for substance abuse, gambling, or spousal battery, or attending to other matters the judge deems important.

Deferred judgments present another option for defendants by delaying the sentencing altogether and placing the defendant on probation for a period of time. If the defendant successfully completes probation, charges are disposed of and that crime is expunged from the person's record.

Accepting Blame Ensures Better Probation Outcome

How well a probationer with ADHD handles probation is largely dependent on the nature of his or her ADHD deficits. For example, consider the defendant who has ADHD of the type that means he blames himself and not others for his problems and this may be his first offense or first formal probation period. Such a defendant often does well with the additional structure that probation provides; the combination of the criminal charge and probation may be exactly what he needs to make necessary life changes.

By contrast, for the person with the type of ADHD that manifest itself in blaming others and resisting authority, probation could prove a complicated disaster. Instead of benefiting from the imposed structure, this ADHD defendant may view all requirements—such as obtaining and maintaining employment, paying restitution, court costs, and attorney fees, or completing substance abuse treatment—as simply "business as usual": meaning other people trying to "control" him. His longstanding rows with parents, teachers, principals, police, and other authority figures grow even more intense toward these new people "assigned to hassle him." His resentment and stubbornness escalate to new heights.

This more difficult probation client usually is non-compliant with basic probationary requirements such as reporting for meetings, keeping a job, attending anger-management classes, paying court-ordered expenses, and undergoing drug, alcohol, or gambling counseling, This makes it very difficult for a probation officer to do even basic case planning, with efforts to rehabilitate seeming futile. Consequently, the ADHD defendant ends up back in court before the same judge who sentenced him and then gave him the opportunity of probation with a record of repeated non-compliance. The probation officer, who typically plays the dual role of counselor/social worker on one hand and police officer on the other, finds the balance tipped entirely into the police officer role. Odds are good that the probation will be revoked and the original sentence imposed.

This probation officer's unique role means that he deals with the defendant more intensively and frequently than anyone else in the criminal justice system (except for staff dealing with incarceration). Therefore, the probation officer is in an ideal position to recognize an undiagnosed ADHD client.

Probation Officer's Clues: Potential Signs of Untreated ADHD

The probation officer should look for the following general behaviors in determining if a person merits ADHD screening:

- They are often late or fail to show up for probation sign-up meetings.
- They ask an excessive number of questions about probation rules and regulations.
- They balk at signing the probation agreement.
- They want to delete certain parts of basic probation agreement terminology that cannot be negotiated.
- Their history reflects trouble in school, related to both disruption and poor academics.

Beyond these generalities, the probation officer will find other clues in the areas of work history, driving and hospital records, and residential history. Remember: Each behavior won't apply to each person with ADHD; the key is identifying a preponderance of behaviors.

<u>Work History</u>
- Defendants with ADHD might have dropped out or barely graduated from high school.
- They probably have a very colorful but short-term employment history. When questioned why jobs didn't last longer, they may say it was due to being late (oversleeping) or just not showing up for work.
- They might have basically told off the boss when corrected for making a mistake.
- They might even claim that they still have a job even though they have not bothered to show up for work for the last week, stating, "I haven't been told I'm fired."

<u>Driving Records and Hospital Visits</u>
- Their driving records are often poor and show many accidents.
- They might have a suspended driver's license and yet still drive right into the probation office parking lot for their sign-up meeting.
- Their criminal records are usually spotted with crimes such as disorderly conduct, resisting arrest, trying to elude law enforcement, failure to appear, assaults, trespassing, and other impulsivity-related crimes.
- Questioning may reveal a history of non-motor vehicle injuries related to risk-taking behavior, acting on dares from peers, or having lots of accidents that resulted in emergency room visits and stitches or broken bones.

Residential Histories and Current Living Situation

- Their residential histories show frequent moves, living with the "friend of the day," being kicked out of the house by parents, then grandparents, then aunts and uncles, and finally their friends.
- Probation agreements usually require prior notification before moving or switching jobs. If the defendant's residential history is sporadic, the probation officer will spend an inordinate amount of time tracking down the probationer. Mail will be returned as "moved no forwarding," and phones will be disconnected.
- Employers will say he hasn't been to work in weeks and is no longer employed.

Tardiness and Disorganization

Routinely, defendants with untreated ADHD show up late for appointments—if they remember at all—forget items they should bring, and show up at the appointment's correct time and day but the wrong month (because they lost or threw away their appointment card as they exited the last meeting). When questioned, they often begin looking for items in their wallet or purse, which resembles an overstuffed filing cabinet.

Based on their past histories, probationers are usually assigned a certain level of supervision regarding how often they must visit their probation officer. Many ADHD defendants may start out in a lower supervision level and, after continued problems, find themselves at the highest level of supervision simply due to their non-compliance—intentional or not.

They will often express as much or more disappointment in themselves than their frustrated probation officer expresses. They may make self-defeating statements such as "I am a loser—always have been and always will be—just ask my teachers and parents." They may get emotional very easily in a probation meeting, especially if they have developed a decent relationship with their probation officer.

They will often come in discouraged, reciting tales of woe and how everything is going badly. Yet by the next meeting, they might come in very excited about this great new job, new girlfriend, or boyfriend that provides the solution to all their problems. The probation officer should try bringing them down to reality in these "high" times and, during the low times, encourage them with positive things they might have done in the past.

Defendants with untreated ADHD frequently tell you that they were always in the principal's office, forced to stay after school for missed schoolwork or disruption, and received detention innumerable times. Suspensions and expulsions from school may have occurred. The fact that probation is not working out well comes as no surprise, they admit. Despite seeming intelligent—often with unusual talents or gifts in areas such as art, acting, music, computers, or mechanical repairs—they manage to constantly sabotage their lives.

Even difficult probation clients still possess likable qualities or are quick to acknowledge some shortcomings. The probation officer may want to give them a break and see how things go. Unfortunately, improvement seldom happens with an ADHD probationer unless the underlying cause (ADHD) is being addressed. As we will see, intermediate sanctions meant to improve compliance—including jail time for contempt of court, being sent to halfway houses, and even prison—seldom work if the probationers have untreated ADHD. Again, that's because ADHD is an issue of brain deficits, not a matter of will.

ADHD and Incarceration: Cellmates, Environment Are Key

Once ADHD offenders enter prison, their environment and cellmates play an important role in their degree of adjustment. If placed in a cellblock with more predator-type criminals, they might become their pawns or else identified as a disturbing influence.

Because they want to show they are as smart or sophisticated as the other prisoners, jail staff may easily catch them showing off or trying to gain acceptance from their cellmates. Depending on their success in adapting, their behavior can lead to confrontation with jail staff or to ridicule and isolation by cellmates. Yet if these same prisoners with ADHD were placed in a cellblock with non-predator or calmer individuals, they may quickly blend in and even be viewed as model prisoners.

Jail and Prison Staff's Clues: Potential Signs of ADHD

If placed in trustee status or in a cellblock with sentenced individuals who are more motivated to stay out of trouble, these ADHD defendants may find that long-needed structure in their lives. The jail staff may consider them likeable, even wondering how or why this person ended up as a prisoner in the first place.

If the untreated ADHD prisoner is one whom jail/prison staff sees frequently—coming in and out of the jail/prison system with some regularity—they might notice a behavior pattern: The individual seems to do better when incarcerated. When released to the outside world, his or her structure breaks down, leading to trouble and a return to jail/prison on new charges. This pattern often repeats itself as the person moves further into the system and into other structured environments within the criminal justice system, such as half-way houses and prison facilities.

What Can Probation Officers and Jail Staff Do?

By recognizing the traits of ADHD—identified above and in previous chapters—and asking questions, including two important ones below, jail staff can identify potential ADHD prisoners and help to break a self-perpetuating cycle of offending.

- "Have you ever been diagnosed with attention deficit hyperactivity disorder?
- The person might have been told earlier in life that he or she has attention deficit hyperactivity disorder, but parents may not have wanted to put their child

on medication. Or the person declined medication.
- "Have you ever been prescribed a medication called Ritalin?"
- The person might have been placed on Ritalin but never told that he or she had ADHD. Positive answers to these questions should be passed on to jail medical staff and the courts.

SUMMARY
- Many opportunities exist for probation officers or jail/prison staff to determine if a probationer or inmate should be referred for ADHD screening.
- Probationary success for a defendant with untreated ADHD depends on the type of deficits the person has. If he tends to blame others for his problems and rebels at any authority, probation will of course go poorly. On the other hand, if he blames himself, the structure that probation provides could help him get his life back on track.
- In Jail/Prison, environment and cellmates play an important role in how well the offender with ADHD adjusts. If placed in a cellblock with more predator-type criminals, they often show off or trying to gain acceptance from their cellmates. Yet if placed in a cellblock with non-predator or calmer individuals, they may quickly blend in and adjust well.
- If staff recognizes that a repeat offender seems to perform better while incarcerated, that could indicate the imposed structure is making up for ADHD deficits that leave the person unable to structure his or her life "on the outside." That person might be a good candidate for ADHD screening.
- Overall, improvement seldom happens with an ADHD defendant until the underlying cause (ADHD) is addressed.

- Few intermediate sanctions meant to improve compliance work if the defendants have untreated ADHD. Again, ADHD is an issue of brain deficits, not a matter of will.

SPINNING OUT OF CONTROL

CHAPTER 7
ADHD Screening and Diagnosis

Previous chapters discussed how criminal justice professionals could better recognize individuals with untreated ADHD in a variety of settings—including at traffic stops, during court proceedings, during probation, and in jails and prisons. This chapter refines recognition by providing a two-step procedure to more positively identify individuals with ADHD in the criminal justice system:

- **Step 1: Screening Appropriately. Learn enough about ADHD to be able to identify defendants likely to have it.**
- **Step 2: Referring for Diagnosis. Understand the components of a proper ADHD evaluation so you can find diagnosticians trained for this specialty.**

Criminal justice professionals can, by learning the common symptoms and behaviors of ADHD defendants, better identify defendants who *might* have ADHD. These professionals are not expected to diagnosis ADHD; they simply are expected to identify everyone who *might* have ADHD and refer them to diagnosing professionals. By casting a wide net, they will be more likely to catch less-obvious cases.

The second step covers referring these defendants who have been screened as likely candidates for an ADHD diagnosis to an expert qualified to conduct a comprehensive evaluation. Not every psychiatrist or psychologist is qualified in this area.

The chapter concludes with two likely scenarios of how an offender might react to the ADHD diagnosis.

Part I: Screening

Casting a Wide Net

A national group of expert researchers and practitioners, meeting at an April 2002 consensus conference, established recommendations for conducting mental-health assessments in the justice system (Wasserman et al., 2003). The most important recommendation: An evidenced-based, scientifically sound screening for all offenders should be conducted as soon as possible. In other words, screen **all** offenders for ADHD.

Before continuing, here is some basic testing terminology. If a testing procedure incorrectly diagnoses an individual with ADHD, it makes a *false positive* mistake. That is, it makes a mistake by saying, "Yes, this person has ADHD." Similarly, if a procedure incorrectly indicates that a person does not have a diagnosis of ADHD; it makes a *false negative* mistake. Namely, it errs by saying, "No, this person does not have ADHD."

The crucial goal of a screening is to ensure that no individual who truly has ADHD will be missed. This means casting a wide net. In this way, the screening process will produce many *false positive* results. In other words, experts conducting evaluations will find that many individuals previously identified as potentially having ADHD do not, in fact, have ADHD. This is perfectly valid and occurs in all screenings for all disorders, psychological or medical. Thus, in a screening, the lethal mistake is to miss referring a true case of ADHD, namely to make a *false negative* mistake. In other words, it's better to suspect that someone *might* have ADHD and refer him or her for an expert diagnosis than to overlook the possibility entirely.

Correctional System Screening Recommendations

As applied to ADHD, the following three screening recommendations maximize the chances of referring everyone who truly has ADHD for expert diagnosis:

1. **Carefully Review Existing Documentation**

Examine all of the offender's existing documentation to see if it includes a prior diagnosis of ADHD. If it does, that indicates an automatic referral to the expert for a confirmatory evaluation.

2. Educate Appropriate Staff in Proper Screening Skills

This book should help staff develop the screening skills necessary to make an appropriate referral. For example, co-author Patrick Hurley was working as a probation officer in 1996 when he learned he had ADHD. During a time when he dealt with approximately 180 probationers, he screened 47 probationers and other persons he knew as possibly having ADHD. Of those 47 screened, experts subsequently diagnosed 46. He still suspects the remaining individual had ADHD but had consulted an inexperienced psychologist.

Hurley also succeeded in encouraging many of his probation clients who had been diagnosed with ADHD earlier in life to resume medication. Some displayed dramatic turnarounds in their lives, especially if they were willing to educate themselves about the disorder. Hurley provides this example:

Jim was on probation for a second offense of driving under the influence of alcohol. He was about 20 years old, involved in college athletics, seemed very bright, and also appeared to want to make improvements in his life. School was proving a struggle, definitely taking a backseat to his desire to be an outstanding athlete. Yet Jim found even athletics problematic, as he was stuck on the second and third team. His single-minded drive to reach the top of his sport probably contributed to his frustrations in life, school, and alcohol abuse.

A fellow probation officer asked me to speak to him about his life in general and, after about 30 minutes of talking with Jim, I felt he was a good candidate for an ADHD evaluation referral. I came to that conclusion because, when I told him about my own experiences and struggles in school, he said he'd like to be doing better in school and knew that he was intelligent enough to do so. He agreed to go in for an evaluation. He was diagnosed with ADHD and prescribed medication, which he took.

Almost immediately, Jim saw improvement in his life and started educating himself on ADHD. A few months later, his probation officer told me that he had quit the athletic team and was devoting his time and efforts to school, with no hesitation about his decision. I later learned that he made the dean's list that semester and the next as well and had no more problems on probation. He was also making restitution payments and would probably be discharged earlier than expected. He told his probation officer that his parents were very happy and proud of him for the first time in his life that was not related to athletic performance. That meant a lot to him. Last I heard, he was discharged early from probation, doing great in school, and enjoying a great outlook on his future.

We believe everyone can develop accurate screening skills if he or she will spend time reading about and studying ADHD, with the result being many more success cases like Jim's. Once the person develops this skill, it won't take long to find possible candidates in the correctional system and then watch them more closely for a period of time. The most delicate part usually is bringing up the issue with the defendant. It is generally best to approach the subject from a different angle, such as telling the person he appears distracted or some other obvious manifestation that the person is likely to confirm. Then it's a matter of waiting to see if the person proves receptive to discussing any problems he might be experiencing. Patrick Hurley found the following questions useful in broaching the subject (more questions can be gathered from books such as Driven to Distraction, which list common behaviors and experiences):

- Did you have academic problems in school as a youngster or excessive discipline problems?
- Did you have difficulty in keeping friends?
- Were you considered to be disruptive or distracted in school?
- Did you have a lot of accidents involving stitches or broken bones?
- Were you the victim of teasing from others? If so how did you handle it?
- Did you have problems with self-esteem?

3. Learn About ADHD Rating Scales

Once you've learned more about the person's history, obtain more information by using evidence-based, scientifically sound ADHD rating scales such as the Conner's scales. These scales are among the best available (Gomez, Walsh, Burns, & Moura, 2003) and may be easily obtaining by contacting the publisher. *(8)* These scales allow an excellent evaluation of the core deficits of ADHD. Administering, scoring, and interpreting the scales for the purposes of screening are simple and straightforward. A training session with an ADHD expert would readily provide the necessary skills for screening.

Part II: Diagnosis

Comprehensive Expert Evaluation for ADHD

Two crucial facts exist with regard to an expert evaluation that may or may not result in an ADHD diagnosis.

No One Test Accurately Diagnoses ADHD

No single test ensures high enough validity for diagnosing ADHD in individuals (American Academy of Pediatrics, 2001; Brown, 2003a). Having ADHD is not like having a broken bone, which can be clearly diagnosed with an X-ray. This is because we can compare ADHD, as you will recall from a prior chapter, to having an impaired orchestra conductor. All the instruments work fine; its how they all work together that is problematic. ADHD involves impaired executive functioning, which involves the integration of numerous cognitive processes. Most tests, however, assess only individual cognitive functions; they do not assess the "orchestra leader" known as executive functioning (Brown, 2003).

This might explain why currently all medical, brain imaging, or neuropsychological tests make far too many mistakes in individual diagnosis (primarily *false negatives*, saying a person doesn't have ADHD when he or she does, in fact, have it) to warrant their use as the sole basis of a diagnosis (American Academy of Pediatrics,

2000; Doyle et al., 2000; Grodzinsky & Barkley, 1999; Loo, 2003; MacDonald, 2003; NIH, 2000). To use the broken-bone analogy again, a properly read X-ray will almost always confirm or disconfirm the physician's diagnosis. Tests for ADHD cannot do this.

The lack of a singularly reliable test for ADHD does not mean that testing is never useful or necessary. For example, in complicated cases that involve not only ADHD but also learning disorders, other neurological disorders, or mental or personality disorders unrelated to ADHD, formal testing can be helpful. Decisions for formal testing can be made only by an expert, which brings us to the second fact.

Accurate Diagnosis Depends on Expertise of Clinician

The single most important element in the diagnosis of ADHD is the expert conducting the evaluation (Brown, 2003a). This point cannot be overemphasized. The "gold standard" procedure for an ADHD diagnosis is an expert who assesses an individual using all of the following four procedures (Brown, 2003a):

• A clinical interview is conducted to garner extensive self-report data from the patient regarding relevant history and current functioning.

• Collateral report data is gathered from multiple sources (parent, teacher, partner, staff, previous evaluations, prior social history information).

• ADHD rating scales such as the Connor's scales, discussed above, are implemented.

• *The Diagnostic and Statistical Manual of Mental Disorders, Fourth Edition, Text Revision* (DSM IV-TR) provides diagnostic criteria supplemented by clinical wisdom and knowledge that overcomes some of the limitations of these criteria. Written primarily for diagnosing ADHD in children, these criteria are limited with regard to the variation in symptoms presented in adults and those with the predominantly inattentive type of ADHD.

Lastly, please note that the foregoing procedures are typical for virtually every diagnosis of any kind of mental disorder. There are no infallible tests, only expert clinical judgment. Hence, every correctional setting must have the services of an expert ADHD diagnostician if the facility hopes to adequately evaluate ADHD. This is especially true with regard to ADHD in the correctional setting because ADHD typically presents with other disorders, making differential diagnosis extremely challenging.

Reactions of Criminal Offenders to an ADHD Diagnosis

Some individuals previously diagnosed with ADHD and prescribed medication may have stopped taking it, for a variety of reasons. Others may receive diagnosis for the first time at this critical problematic time in their lives. To some who are diagnosed, this comes as "good news." It gives them a name to help explain some of their problems in life (not an excuse, just pieces of the jigsaw puzzle of their lives coming into place). This type of person will usually go to counseling, take his recommended medications, and cooperate with those trying to help him. Witness the example of Justin:

Justin is 20 years old and on probation for theft after undercharging his friends for items at the clothing department store where he worked. In fact, this was an ongoing situation, where Justin would ring up one shirt for his friends and put four pairs of slacks or jeans and four other shirts they'd selected into the bag and let them leave. It was only after these friends told their friends about it, who then came in to try it, that Justin got caught.

Justin appears friendly and bright. He expressed remorse about his shoplifting scheme, which he knew was wrong and, more importantly, about disappointing his parents.

Justin had been diagnosed with ADHD in his sophomore year of high school. At that point, he took medication. His scores did improve a little in his junior and senior years. Justin said he stopped taking medication about two months before he graduated because he didn't like the idea of taking it and didn't really feel it helped him, even though his parents said they could always tell when he had or hadn't taken it.

Justin is polite and has expressed a desire to complete probation successfully and have a better life. He felt he got started on the theft scam at the suggestion of one of his so-called friends. He liked the kid and looked up to him and had always struggled with keeping friends. This boy ended up being no friend to Justin. Justin got in over his head and feared that if he didn't continue, one of them might report him.

Justin started community college and wants to get his four-year degree. When asked what he knows about ADHD, he admitted he knew almost nothing. The probation officer reviewed with Justin why ADHD may have contributed to his troubles. He told him it is not an excuse but that addressing the ADHD matter proactively could improve his chances at completing probation early, doing better in school, and getting better control of his life. He encouraged him to read a few books on the subject

On the next visit, Justin came in and said he read several of the books and felt like they could have been written about him. The books explained the disorder in a more positive manner than he had thought of it before. Voluntarily, Justin went back to his doctor and re-started his medicine. He found more books on the subject and planned to attend a support group.

Justin reported that the medicine seems to be helping. His girlfriend said he seems more focused and involved. Justin promised his probation officer he would continue to work on learning more about how ADHD affects his life. The probation officer says he is very optimistic that Justin will do well on probation.

Justin's is a "good news" story. To other people with ADHD, however, news of diagnosis comes as the "worst news" they have ever received. These are characterized as persons who have always blamed others for their problems, especially parents, daycare providers, teachers, principals, police, and other authority figures. To accept this diagnosis would mean "looking in the mirror" at themselves. This is unacceptable and so they resist counseling, taking medication, and other efforts of those trying to help them. The outcomes for success for this second group are seldom positive.

Unless or until they accept the basic fact that they have to live with their behavior and those negative aspects associated with them, their future will most likely be filled with more of the same frustrations and problems. Here's an example:

John, 22, is on probation for residential burglary. Past charges, though less serious, haunt him as well. Diagnosed with ADHD when he was 8 years old, John took medication off and on until he started high school, when he stopped. He says he was "tired of people trying to control my behavior with mind-altering drugs."

John, according to his pre-sentence investigation report, dropped out of school sophomore year and has not obtained a GED. He has had so many jobs he cannot remember them all—mostly short-term, minimum-wage jobs. John said he didn't get along with his bosses; it was their fault that he quit or was fired because all of them were unreasonable.

At his first appointment, John tested positive for both marijuana and cocaine. He has been ordered in for a substance abuse evaluation, which five weeks later he still has not obtained. He said he is still working at the fast food restaurant, a job he started a few days before probation began, five weeks ago, but he has no pay stubs to prove it.

John said that he and his boss don't get along because he has been late a few times and the boss has "jumped on him" about it. Further questioning reveals that John stays up until 3:00 a.m. or 4:00 a.m. and has trouble awakening in time to make it to work by 11:00 a.m. He says he has always been a "night owl."

He said he is working "maybe 15 to 20" hours per week. Asked why he can't work more hours, he again blames his boss and says that he was promised more hours but the boss dropped his hours after he was late a couple times. With John present, the probation officer called to John's employer. His boss said John's last day was two weeks ago, when he failed to show up. After John failed to return the boss's phone calls, he removed John from the active roster. When asked if he would consider John an employee, he said, "Absolutely not," and he was not going to be rehired.

When confronted with this information, John accused his former boss of being a liar. He said his boss never told him he was fired and he never quit, so as far as John is concerned he still works there (even though he hadn't shown up for work in more than two weeks and had not returned his boss's telephone calls).

The probation officer asks John why he is not addressing his ADHD problem. He said he doesn't want to take mind-altering drugs. When told he has already tested positive for marijuana and cocaine and these are illegal mind-altering drugs, he said those are drugs he has chosen to take and not drugs other people want him to take.

John is in trouble on his probation very quickly. His probation officer now requires John to receive substance abuse evaluation and visit a community mental health doctor. He must learn if he can get back on medication for his ADHD because many doctors are reluctant to prescribe stimulant medications to known drug abusers.

John learns that if he fails to comply with getting a job, ceasing illegal drug use, and participating in substance abuse treatment and ADHD recommendations, he can expect to go back before the judge very soon for a contempt of court or possible revocation of probation hearing. Based on John's body language and reaction to this news, the probation officer is not optimistic of John's ultimate success on probation.

SUMMARY

If correctional settings heed the recommendations from the panel of expert researchers and practitioners, they will implement excellent screening procedures and referrals to mental-health professionals who are expert at diagnosing ADHD. If offenders diagnosed with ADHD are then amenable to receiving proper treatment, correctional institutions will enjoy many more successes.

CHAPTER 8
Treatment for ADHD

Treatment for ADHD typically takes place in three ways: Medical; psychological/educational; and coaching/educational

These treatment methods can be combined and tailored to meet the individual needs of the person with ADHD. When properly implemented, these approaches prove highly successful for those in the correctional system, as case histories in this chapter illustrate.

Indeed, in many ways, case-history success stories comprise the heart of this book because they illustrate *the* reason for writing this book: Namely, a solid understanding of ADHD can lead to a proper referral, correct diagnosis, and highly successful treatment. *Correct* treatment of individuals with ADHD by the *correctional system* can dramatically change a person's life for the better, as the case history of "David" in Chapter 2 showed. The *wobbly top* can be put on the right course.

Read, study, and watch. You never know when you might be able to turn someone's life around.

Medical Treatment
How did medical science discover that a stimulant medicine would lessen a person's hyperactivity and not, as logic might dictate, make him more hyperactive? As with many profoundly important scientific discoveries, the answer is *dumb luck!*

Charles Bradley, fresh out of his residency in 1937, accepted a position as medical director at the Emma Pendleton Bradley Home for Children in Providence, Rhode Island. Many of the children in the hospital were victims of encephalitis and other well-established sources of neurological damage. A primitive, now extinct procedure termed a *pneumo-encephalogram* was a common way to document brain injury. This procedure often caused severe headaches, and Bradley believed that a stimulant drug like Benzedrine might reduce these headaches. After the first week of instituting Benzedrine treatment, about half of the 30 children receiving Benzedrine showed a "spectacular change in behavior and remarkably improved school performance." The classroom teachers at the hospital noted an increased zest for learning among the children, dubbing the medicine "arithmetic pills" (Connors, 2000).

For some time afterwards, this astonishing finding was termed a *paradoxical* effect, because a so-called stimulant medicine calmed rather than intensified hyperactivity. We now know that with ADHD, certain brain circuits are actually under-active (MacDonald, 2003), and, as previously indicated, most probably there is a lower level of the brain chemicals norepinepherine and dopamine. Hence, stimulants do exactly what they are supposed to do: increase the levels of dopamine and norepinepherine, thereby *stimulating*, or activating, the under-active brain circuits. The slowing, wobbly top starts spinning the way it should. The effect is not paradoxical but logical.

More specifically, there are two major effects. First there is an increase in the signal-to-noise ratio such that task-specific signals are enhanced, background random noise signals are decreased, and thus *selective attention* is increased. In other words, stimulant medication acts like someone tuning a radio signal: the station comes in loud and clear but static is eliminated. Second, there is an increase in significance of a task to an individual, thus making the task more interesting and improving *sustained attention* (Volkow, cited in Imperio & Anderson, 2004).

As a consequence of Bradley's discovery, the international consensus of the best and the brightest scientists working in the field of ADHD, citing hundreds of scientific studies, has established the remarkable short-term and long-term effectiveness of medical treatment for ADHD for children (Ambroggio & Jensen, 2002; Barkley, 2002b; Biederman, 2003), with the more severe cases benefiting even more (Teicher et al., 2003). What exactly is a scientific study that provides evidence that a treatment for ADHD is effective? The gold standard for evaluating treatment effectiveness for both medical and psychological treatments is what is termed a *random assignment, placebo-controlled, double- blind study*. This mouthful of terms means that subjects are randomly assigned to three groups: active treatment, no treatment, placebo (fake or bogus treatment such as sugar pills). Furthermore, the subjects in the treatment and placebo groups as well as the individuals assessing the effectiveness of treatment are *blinded*. In other words, both subjects and researchers don't know who is receiving which treatment until the treatment is over. This methodology allows scientists to conclude that the medication caused the improvement as opposed to psychological factors such as a person's high hopes.

Thanks to hundreds of scientific studies, even the mainstream popular press is finally beginning to acknowledge what the scientific community has long known, as evidenced by the following editorial excerpt, entitled "Ritalin's Gift" from the *Chicago Tribune* newspaper (1/8/03). In the words of Dr. Mina Dulcan, chief of child and adolescent psychiatry at Northwestern University Medical School:

"There's a lot of nonscientific thrashing about in this area, and there are some people who are simply opposed to psychiatry's use of medicine. We're trying to treat these kids, and we've got people running around scaring patients. The evidence that stimulants work, that they help people, and that they are not dangerous is overwhelming."

Lastly, note that although there are far fewer scientific studies on adolescents and adults with ADHD, the existing studies (all of which are of short-term effectiveness, such as a month) find medication to be an equally effective treatment (National Resource Center for ADHD, 2004).

Innumerable case examples illustrate the *overwhelming scientific evidence* for medication's effectiveness. The following serves as well as any, being a recollection of the writer's experience as a schoolchild with ADHD, untreated until the fourth grade:

Whatever concentration I had for an in-class assignment was gone by the fifth problem. Sometimes I would be so distracted, I couldn't even start on my work. It was not deliberate, and it was not something I could control. I just could not pay attention to the task. The tapping of a pencil by another student or the rustling of papers would instantly take my mind off what I was supposed to be doing. After the distraction would pass, I could turn back to the class work. That lasted about 10 seconds before something else would call my mind away from what I was supposed to be doing. Before I knew it, the work was due and I had to rush to fill in any answer I could pull out of the air.

From my head to my toes, I could feel every little thing. I could feel if the part in my hair was not straight. I had to rip off all the tags on my shirts right away, because even that two-inch piece of fabric could cause me to fail a test. If shoes were even slightly too tight or too loose, it became more important to me to fix them than take the test. I could not concentrate. I knew I should pay attention, but even the effort of paying attention became another distraction.

In fourth grade, I experienced sweet relief; I was prescribed Ritalin. It worked wonders. I felt so much better. All the little things that used to drive me nuts were gone. I felt much more mature and calm. My work was much better. My test grades improved. The little distractions that called me away all through the day faded. It was an endless loop, and one little pill took that entire burden off a child's shoulders. (This is an edited version of a letter to the Chicago Tribune [1/9/03].)

Once again, it is quite simple. Overwhelming scientific evidence shows there is a highly effective medical treatment for ADHD. All reasonable persons accept the obvious fact that highly effective medical treatments exist for many medical disorders. Even so, nonscientific thrashing continues to exist, perhaps primarily in those who are unfamiliar with the disorder and the treatment. Another reason is lack of education. Answers to these frequently asked questions should help dispel lingering confusion on the topic.

Frequently Asked Questions About Medical Treatment

Q: What are the different kinds of medicine used to treat ADHD?

The first-tier medications for treating ADHD include a variety of short-acting (3-4 hours) and longer-acting (6-12 hours) stimulants and one non-stimulant medication. There are two kinds of stimulant medications: methylphenidate based and amphetamine based (Biederman, 2003). At the time of this writing, the major medications are as follows:

Methylphenidate-Based Medications
- *Short-acting*: *Ritalin, Generic Methylphenidate, Focalin*
- *Longer-acting*: *Methylphenidate SR 20, Ritalin SR, Metadate ER, Methylin ER, Metadate CD, Concerta*

Amphetamine-Based Medications
- *Short-acting*: *Adderall Tablet, Dexedrine Tablet*
- *Longer-acting*: *Dexedrine Spansule, Adderall XR*

Non-Stimulant Medication
- *Atomoxetine (Strattera)*

Q: Which medication is the best?

All medications affect the same neural networks (Newcorn, 2003) and appear to be equally effective based upon group data. For any one individual, however, one medication might work much more effectively than another. For example, for 50 percent of children, Ritalin and Dexedrine are equally effective, but for 20 percent, Ritalin is more effective and for 30 percent, Dexedrine is more effective (Biederman, 2003). Because there is no way to predict this differential responsiveness in advance or what the best dose is, the only sure way of determining which medication to use is trial and error (Pliszka et al.; Rabiner, 2003).

Q: Are there still other medications? I've heard of treatment with medications that are typically prescribed for depression, for example, Tofranil, Norpramine, and Wellbutrin?

Stimulant medications are the first-line treatment for ADHD for children, adolescents, and adults (Biederman, 2003; National Resource Center for ADHD, 2004). In the most substantial research to date on optimal effective medical treatment for ADHD, termed the *Multimodal Treatment Study (MTA)*, less than 2 percent of the children were treated with non-stimulant medications or multiple medications (Rabiner, 2003). Thus, optimal medical treatment almost never requires multiple medications or treatment with non-stimulants (some kind of anti-depressant, for example).

Unfortunately, as many as 25 percent of children treated in community settings who receive stimulant treatment are also prescribed a second medication. This is highly problematic because the safety and efficacy of combined pharmacotherapy with ADHD has not been established (Rabiner, 2003). **(Editors Note:** *Co-Author Patrick Hurley disagrees with this opinion as he has been on Prozac for the entire time he has been on Ritalin and knows that the two medications work well in tandem; in addition many of the persons who come to his support groups are being treated by their doctors with stimulants and anti-depressants)*The American Academy of Pediatrics (2001) clearly indicated in its clinical practice guidelines that: "The use of non-stimulant medications falls outside this practice guideline" (p. 13).

It is important to note, however, that second-line medications such as Tofranil, Norpramine, and Wellbutrin are sometimes used in cases where there is an incomplete response or no response to stimulant treatment. More commonly, however, these medications are used to treat co-existing disorders in adults because approximately two-thirds to three-quarters of adults with ADHD also have at least one other psychological disorder in their lifetime (National Resource Center for ADHD, 2004). As yet there are no "gold standard" scientific studies on medication therapy in adults with ADHD and co-existing disorders (National Resource Center for ADHD, 2004). Hence the treatment decision is based upon clinical experience (National Resource Center for ADHD, 2004).

Q: How long does it take to achieve an optimal medical regimen?

The onset of the effect of medications is somewhat varied but can be almost immediate—that is, within a half hour, especially when a short-acting medication is taken on an empty stomach. An optimal regimen can typically be achieved within one or two months when working with an expert who adjusts the medication on a weekly basis.

Q: As a young person grows, will the dosing regimen need to be changed?

This book is for everyone in the correctional system, which includes children and adults, so this is an important question. In addition, because ADHD is not something that develops in adulthood but has been present in an individual since childhood, we will mention some children-related studies as they apply to adults as well.

Most probably, especially if there are different developmental demands with regard to functioning (Brown, 2003), the dosing regimen will need occasional adjustment. Note, however, that there is not a tolerance buildup. In other words, the person will not need to take larger and larger amounts of the medication to achieve the same effect (Biederman, 2003). But there will be cases where an increased dosage may be needed.

Far less research exists on adult ADHD. Yet one of the leading experts on pharmacological treatment of ADHD, Dr. Joseph Biederman (2003), has affirmed that existing research, limited as it is, indicates that stimulant treatment for ADHD in adults is essentially as effective as it is for children and adolescents, provided the doctor knows what he or she is doing,

So, the good news is that what is effective for pediatric ADHD is also effective for adult ADHD. Most of what applies to children in terms of diagnosing and treating the disorder also works well with adults.

Q: Will a child need to take medication forever?

For those 65 percent of children who will continue to have impairing symptoms into adulthood, the answer is most probably *yes*.

However, even in the 65 percent of cases, much depends on the demands of the person's daily life as well as the coping and compensatory mechanisms he or she has developed. A person will need to take medication for as long as it is required for them to properly function in different areas of life. In some cases, people seem to outgrow the major problems with the disorder or learn how to compensate or adapt. On the other hand, some people only think they have adapted when in fact they could probably still use medication in order to be higher functioning. It's very individualistic.

Q: How is it that about 35 percent of people apparently "grow out" of ADHD?

No one knows for sure, but a normalization of neurotransmitter levels or brain volumes may occur (Farone, 2003). In these cases, it may mean that a certain portion of childhood onset may simply be a developmental delay (Castellanos, 1997; 2000) and less genetically influenced (Farone, 2000).

Q: Aren't there serious short-term side effects to the medication? How common are they? How long do they last?

As with every medication, there are some side effects such as insomnia, reduced appetite, stomachache, headache, or dizziness (Pliszka et al., 2002). With stimulants, the good news is that typically about 36 percent of the children do not experience side effects. When they do, the side effects are usually minor, of short duration, and easily rectified with dosage adjustments (Pliszka et al; Rapport & Moffitt, 2002).

Q: What about long-term adverse effects of medication?

Historically there have been two major concerns: reduced adult height and possible development of a permanent tic disorder. Scientific research has concluded that concern is not justified regarding possible tic-disorder development (Tourette's Syndrome Study Group, 2002), but medication may have an adverse effect on height. In the most comprehensive study to date, children with ADHD aged from 7 to 9 who were continuously medicated for two years grew about one-half inch less than the national average for this two-year period (Jensen et al, 2003). Only time will tell if this growth pattern continues. Furthermore, because of the study's limitations, it is possible that the growth suppression effect was due to factors other than treatment with medication (MTA Cooperative Group, 2004a).

What are the implications then of this tentative, worrisome finding? First, as with all medications, one must make a risk/benefit analysis. Are the positive effects worth the trade-off with this *possible* negative side effect? Second, as often as possible, the lowest possible effective dosage should be administered, and, whenever feasible, the patient should take holidays from medication treatment. For example, parents need to evaluate whether or not medication is really needed when their child is not in school or doing homework (MTA Cooperative Group, 2004a).

In terms of other possible long-term effects, the fact that methylphenidate and dextroamphetamine have been in clinical use for more than 60 years makes it highly improbable that any new medical risk from treatment with stimulant medication will emerge (Pliszka et al.).

Q: Aren't stimulants being horrendously over-prescribed? Aren't we engaging in a wholesale chemical muzzling of America's youth?

The partial answer is yes. Apparent instances of over-prescription of stimulant medication exist—for example, 20 percent of white fifth-grade boys in one community (Olfson, Gameroff, Marcus, & Jensen, 2003). This, of course, only means that some medical professionals are more likely to place someone on medication based on a teacher or school recommendation without conducting the proper evaluation.

The "big picture" answer, however, is no, stimulants are not being over-prescribed. The proportion of children with ADHD who receive any kind of treatment varies widely by community, with rates ranging from 12.5 percent to 68 percent (Olfson, Gameroff, Marcus, & Jensen, 2003). In other words, anywhere from 32 to 87.5 percent of children with ADHD are *not* receiving treatment.

Furthermore, the average medically treated child with ADHD receives only about two prescriptions per year (Jensen, 2000). Note that because stimulants such as Ritalin are classified as a Schedule II drug, refills cannot be written with the initial prescription nor can refills be called in to pharmacies. Patients must be given written prescriptions. An average of two prescriptions per year means that the average child with ADHD is most probably being under-medicated.

Q: Are other medical or quasi-medical treatments effective—for example, acupuncture, amino acid supplementation, and EEG biofeedback?

Comprehensive reviews of these treatments concluded that there is no solid evidence of effectiveness as determined by "gold standard" studies (Arnold, 2002; Barkley, 2004; Loo, 2003; 2004).

There may be a one exception to the rule, however. For some children, the symptoms of ADHD may be caused by certain food sensitivities that can be effectively treated by following a stringent diet (Arnold, 2002). Note that the percentage of children with

ADHD who have a food sensitivity or the percentage of children with a food sensitivity who have ADHD symptoms has not been established scientifically, but it is certainly a tiny minority, perhaps about 5 percent (Arnold, 2002).

Q: So then is stimulant medication a panacea?

Of course not. No reasonably educated person has ever said so. It is a remarkably effective medical treatment for a medical developmental disorder.

Q: What then is the role, if any, for psychosocial treatments?

First, the role of psychosocial treatments is that of an addendum to medical treatment for a medical disorder. Stimulant medicine is the first line of treatment, and it is more effective than exclusive psychosocial interventions (Ambroggio & Jensen, 2002; Biederman, 2003; Farone, 2003; Jensen et al., 2003). For example, in the most important, comprehensive treatment study to date, the *MTA* study, *(9)* when exclusive state-of-the-art, comprehensive, intensive psychosocial interventions were compared to optimal medical management alone, medical management proved superior, especially for ADHD symptoms and oppositional/aggressive behaviors (Jensen et al., 2003). Furthermore, when these state-of-the-art, comprehensive, intensive psychosocial interventions were added to optimal stimulant treatment for children, there was no increase in treatment effectiveness for the core symptoms of ADHD and oppositional/aggressive behaviors, as compared to medical treatment alone (Arnold et al., 2004).

Combined treatment, however, offered slightly greater benefits than medication alone for some domains such as peer relations, parent-child relations, and academic outcomes (Jensen et al., 2003). This is quite an achievement for medication and should come as no surprise since ADHD is not the result of faulty learning but of a biologically based deficiency (Barkley, 2000b). Moreover, note that the modest advantages of adding psychosocial treatment to medical treatment were attained by treatments much more intense than most outpatient programs offer (Arnold et al., 2004).

Second, 10 months after the study ended, those children who had been assigned to the optimal medication treatment group and continued medical treatment with a community physician of their choice, continued to experience virtually the same benefits of treatment for ADHD and oppositional/defiant symptoms, as they had when the study ended (MTA Cooperative Group, 2004b).

Third, the foregoing conclusions are all based on group data and, of course, treatment always involves individuals. Hence, in any individual case, especially those cases that involve other co-morbid disorders, inept parenting practices, or several decades of the faulty learning of bad habits, the addition of a psychological intervention may be appropriate and necessary.

Finally, try the following analogy. Think of a person with ADHD as someone whose house is on fire and filled with smoke. It is impossible to evaluate the structural damage to the house until the fire is quenched and the smoke is clear. In ADHD, optimal medical treatment puts out the fire and clears the smoke. Once this occurs, structural damage can be more accurately determined—that is, the remaining problems can be assessed and interventions initiated. Furthermore, it is simply astounding how much of the impaired functioning is not *structural damage* (that is, faulty learning) but the *fog/smoke of ADHD,* as indicated by the marked improvements that can take place when one is able to *do* what one knows one can and should do.

The Role of ADHD Coaching

Coaching is a newer concept to the field of ADHD and is an intervention focused on those aspects of impairment that remain after the person has responded to optimal medical treatment. ADHD coaches are normally not licensed therapists (although there are many who are). The ADHD coach may or may not be appropriate for a criminal defendant, depending on the circumstances, but is certainly worth consideration at any time in the process from time of arrest to disposition of the case. Effective coaching requires the client to be willing to assist the coach in working on problem areas. This is often not the case for a large number of criminal defendants. Many others, however, do acknowledge that they struggle with their ADHD symptoms and may be ideal candidates for referral to a coach early on in the criminal justice process.

How does one work with an ADHD coach?

ADHD coaches work with their clients on life skills and goal setting as well as accountability. Their focus with the client is usually on helping identify strengths and weaknesses and using the strengths to help with the weak areas, which may include:

- Organization
- Keeping appointments with attorneys and court dates
- Maintaining employment
- Impulsiveness
- Relationships
- Procrastination
- Prioritization

Coaches normally engage not in therapy but rather in talking through areas the client considers to be both important to him and where he feels he is falling short in his obligations to himself, his family, or society. The best analogy is that the coach serves in a similar fashion as a probation officer, with the difference being that the client is not legally obligated to meet with a coach. The coach and client agree on areas that need work, set agreeable deadlines for accomplishing them, and then the coach follows up with the client to make sure goals are attained.

The ADHD client normally is accustomed to having a friend, relative, parent, or spouse serve as someone that "stays on top of him." Because it is vital to ADHD clients to maintain these relationships, transferring accountability to a third-party such as a coach can relieve this burden on the close significant other. The coach can serve as the sounding board, with frustrations and anger given vent in an appropriate manner without affecting these close relationships. Obviously, if the client is in prison or on probation or parole, there are people who are obligated to serve in the coaching role, and coaching would probably be neither practical nor useful except in some rare cases.

Case-History Success Stories in the Correctional System

The following case-history success stories comprise the heart of this book, for they illustrate why we wrote this book: A solid understanding of ADHD can lead to a proper referral, correct diagnosis, and successful treatment. And that of course is what *corrections* is all about. *Correct* treatment of ADHD can dramatically change a person's life for the better. The histories are drawn from the approximately 180 probation cases co-author Patrick Hurley saw after he was diagnosed with ADHD.

Susan: Driving Under the Influence

Susan was 26 years old when placed on minimum probation for one year for operating a vehicle under the influence of alcohol. Minimum probation required her to come into the probation office to fill out a quick probation sign-up sheet, stay out of trouble for a year, and perform 20 hours of community service. She had to file monthly reports and pay fines and court costs. Usually these types of clients can be discharged in the seventh or eighth month of probation if they have completed everything. Susan, however, did not have to come into the office again until it was time to send the discharge recommendation in. I had talked to her several times after six months about getting her court costs and fines paid and doing her community service and she kept telling me she was sorry and had been procrastinating.

By the ninth month, she still had done nothing, and I was willing to discharge her early if she would complete things. She agreed to complete them within one month. After the tenth month, I contacted her to express displeasure with her performance and ask that she visit my office. Prior to her appointment, she took care of the court costs and fines but had not set up a place to perform her community service work.

At this point, I talked with Susan for a while and asked her to tell me about her life. I found out that she had been in psychiatric counseling for about six years. The more I talked to her about things in her life and what she struggled with, such as procrastination and relationship issues, I became convinced that she might have ADHD. I asked her if her psychiatrist had ever tested her for it or pursued that option. She told me no and that someone when she was a child had suggested she get evaluated for it but she and her parents never followed through.

I explained to her some of my struggles with ADHD, which made her sit up straight in her chair and look at me with eyes wider open. She had many, many questions. After about two hours, she said that the things we had talked about were exactly on point with her own struggles in life and she wanted more information. I recommended Sari Solden's book Women with ADD, and she said she would go to the bookstore immediately after leaving my office. She also said she was going to speak to her psychiatrist about this.

The next morning I received a call from an excited Susan, who had purchased the book and stayed up most of the night finishing it. She said she had never read a book cover to cover in her life and related to me that it was almost like reading an autobiography of her own life and frustrations. She wanted me to know she had called her psychiatrist and gotten an appointment to speak to him on this matter and she had called the place where we agreed she would do her community service work. She also asked for the names of more books she could read on the subject.

About a week and half later, I received another call from Susan advising that her psychiatrist had placed her on stimulant medication and she had a great response to it. She told me she would be finishing her 20 hours of community service the next day and immediately would bring to me the signed form that was necessary. She also asked if I would have some time to talk to her and I told her I did.

The following day she appeared with her completed community service sheet and began telling me all of the books she had read (all the ones I had recommended) and began thanking me almost to the point of embarrassment for helping her to turn her life around. She said that she had been seeing the psychiatrist for six years and in that time had gained a lot of coping tools but had never learned the underlying cause. She told me that my visit with her and the readings she did on her own and what she had proven to herself in the last week and a half had shown her what potential she had in her life for the first time.

Susan planned to continue seeing her psychiatrist for a while but said she did not anticipate the need to keep going to him much longer. She said that the discovery that she had ADHD had empowered her more than anything else had in her life. I practically had to kick her out of the office to get my work done. That was a very rewarding meeting for me personally and professionally. I discharged her probation that day. It then seemed fortuitous that she had failed to comply with her probation's simple requirements, forcing me to call her into the office that day. Between the time she had signed up for probation to that day of our meeting, I had learned about my own ADHD, meaning I was able to help a person who so desperately was looking for answers.

Ben: Delivery of Cocaine

Ben, 32, was a semi-professional on probation for delivery of Schedule 1 controlled substance: cocaine. Ben was working and paying court costs and fines, but he continued to struggle with cocaine abuse. His urinalysis for cocaine came back positive on several occasions, forcing me to send him back for more drug treatment He was on a beeline back to court for violations of his probation.

Strangely enough, when Ben would stop using cocaine while in treatment (and under the pressure of going to jail), his work life seemed to deteriorate. He was arriving late and not doing as well on the job. He also wasn't making his court cost payments on time.

In talking with Ben (a very likable guy), I directed the conversation to his past as well as his current situation and frustrations. He wanted to kick the cocaine habit and wanted to be successful on probation. He was struggling with both. At the same time, he wanted to be successful at his sales career but that seemed to take a dip anytime he stopped using cocaine. After several discussions with Ben about the possibility of his having ADHD, he agreed that it seemed he had many of the classic characteristics and we referred him for an evaluation.

Ben phoned me after the evaluations and told me he had learned that he had a substantially above average IQ and that the psychologist thought that he did have ADHD. They were trying to find a medical doctor who might be willing to prescribe him a dose of legal stimulant medication. After some major struggles and writing a letter, we finally got the doctor to write a prescription and I agreed to step up my already intense drug screening of Ben.

Ben made a dramatic turnaround. He never had another positive urinalysis test while on probation. He paid all his court costs and fees and was doing well in his professional and personal life when I last saw him. He was discharged from probation eight months earlier than the original three-year probation term.

Seth: Residential Burglary

Seth, 18, was a recent high school graduate placed on three years of probation for burglary of a residence. Seth entered probation with a big chip on his shoulder and was rather defiant from the outset. During his intake appointment, I told him I was going to take a routine drug screen and he protested loudly that he was not on probation for drug use but for burglary. Naturally, this sent up a major red flag to me that he was probably abusing illegal drugs. Sure enough, the drug screen came back positive for marijuana.

Seth wanted to relocate to get a job; for me to make a recommendation for him to do so, I would have to get his probation rules and requirements well underway. He was not happy when I told him he would have to go in for a substance abuse evaluation and comply with any recommended treatment they suggested. Because I would have had to transfer his case to another probation office, I was not willing to let him go until we resolved this issue.

Seth went in for an evaluation and they recommended that he receive out-patient treatment. *During this time, the treatment facility and I were both doing urinalysis testing, and Seth continued to have positive tests for marijuana after several months. At almost every meeting with me, Seth expressed his displeasure with being forced to stay here when he had some job offers lined up elsewhere. I continued to express my displeasure with his non-compliance with probation by continuing to use marijuana and pointed out that he could be going back to court if his behavior continued and possibly do some jail time for contempt of court or be sent to a half-way house.*

During one of our calmer meetings, Seth and I talked about his personal life in more depth and I felt that he might be a good candidate for an ADHD evaluation. Seth said one of his teachers had suggested years earlier that he be checked, but no follow-up was ever done. I told Seth that if he went in voluntarily for an evaluation I would agree to hold off for now on sending him back to court. Seth agreed to do this and after two missed appointments and another stern discussion, he finally went in for the evaluation.

He called me after the evaluation, advising me that the psychologist felt Seth had ADHD. The fact that Seth was undergoing substance abuse treatment at the time again made it difficult to locate a doctor who would prescribe Seth a sample dose of medication for follow-up testing. Seth was not the most cooperative person in advocating on his own behalf or following up, so it was up to me and the psychologist to do most of the searching for a doctor who would agree.

Finally a doctor agreed to prescribe a sample dose of Ritalin and Seth was tested again after taking the medication. Seth showed dramatic improvement on his test and called me the next day and, for the first time, seemed to show some optimism that he could get his life in order. The doctor allowed Seth to begin taking Ritalin, and I saw a dramatic improvement in his attitude, work ethic, and cooperation with probation and substance abuse treatment. Seth seemed to be excited that he had found out about ADHD and began having negative urinalysis test for the first time. After several months, Seth dropped the idea of moving away and found a more stable job and completed substance abuse treatment. He had also read about ADHD.

I was almost to the point where I would stop running such frequent urinalysis test on him. About a month later I decided I would run one. Seth, prior to testing, confessed to me that he had "screwed up." I asked him if he was smoking pot again and he said, "No, not that." He then explained that he had read that some people might be self-medicating themselves by using methamphetamine, cocaine, and other drugs. Since he had such a dramatic outcome with Ritalin, he thought he would try some methamphetamine to see if it would help even more. I had to restrain myself by remembering I was dealing with an 18-year-old. Sure enough, he tested positive for methamphetamine.

I was forced to send Seth back in for further substance evaluation and he was again ordered to undergo outpatient treatment. I also forced him to advise his doctor about this use of methamphetamine and have his doctor contact me. I told Seth he could very well have jeopardized his legitimate use of Ritalin by making such a foolish error. Naturally, Seth had never thought about this possibility. Even though I had told him that continuing to use marijuana after being prescribed Ritalin could jeopardize things, he never made the connection to abusing some other drug. I told Seth he would have to plead his own case to his doctor and that if asked I would recommend that he be allowed to stay on Ritalin. I also sent Seth back to court and recommended he be given as an intermediate sanction, five days in the county jail for contempt of court for his earlier drug abuse of marijuana and this recent incident with methamphetamine.

Seth agreed to do the five days for contempt of court without a fight in court and assured me he would not mess up again. Seth completed his treatment, did his 5 days and was discharged successfully on probation 10 months early on his 3-year probation. I see him from time to time, and he always thanks me for my help and tells me that life is going well. He is continuing his medication.

SUMMARY

Optimal treatment with stimulant medication is the gold standard of treatment for ADHD and is markedly effective at least 70 percent of the time (Biederman, 2003; Wilens, 2003). The word *optimal* is used quite advisedly because the typical medical treatment for this disorder is non-optimal and hence less effective than what it can be (Biederman, 2003).

As for the role of therapy, the first line of treatment for a medical disorder such as ADHD is a highly effective medical treatment, *not* a psychosocial intervention. This in no way is meant to denigrate the appropriate role of psychological treatments, but it is meant to acknowledge the obvious, which has been supported by overwhelming scientific data.

CHAPTER 9
Conclusion

The criminal justice system consists of many different organizations and responsibilities. Helping each to identify and refer ADHD clients requires an overall educational approach. We conclude this book by reviewing the role various criminal-justice professionals can play in screening for ADHD.

Police officers on the street have little initial contact time with a potential ADHD client. Yet the ability to detect common ADHD behaviors—such as blowing an incident out of proportion and having a car full of disorganized junk—could lead the officer to ask this question: "Have you ever been diagnosed with attention deficit Hyperactivity disorder or been prescribed Ritalin?" A criminal investigation might allow more contact, and that might give the officer a better sense of the person. From there, the officer could make a suggestion or include information in the report.

Jail personnel have limited contact, too. The clues to look for would be the wallet or packrat-type backpack stuffed with bits of paper, old lottery tickets, receipts from convenience stores that are months old for buying a bag of chips and a Mountain Dew. Perhaps some of the other traits mentioned in the book will stand out with the education and further knowledge of ADHD. Jail personnel could make a referral or the jail could have a brochure available to hand out or put in inmates' property bags suggesting they get checked.

Pre-trial interviewers have a chance to notice the many job changes or frequent changes of address. They also can call references to ask about the person's stability, and these references might reveal that the person is very dysfunctional. The interviewers could suggest a referral for ADHD evaluation.

Judges may see the same person repeatedly: a beaten down individual who just keeps messing up. Judges could include ADHD brochures in the court paperwork documents.

Defense attorneys obviously get to know their clients and are in a position to ask about past treatments and recommend getting an evaluation.

Prosecutors might also see these clients repeatedly and make the recommendation to the defense attorney that clients should be evaluated. This should not be seen as trying to help the defense get an excuse for the client's misconduct. We do not believe ADHD should be used as an excuse. Making the referral, however, could be the right thing to do for society, for taxpayers, and for the individual.

Pre-trial supervisors, if such supervision is ordered, could require as a condition that the person be evaluated and a report filed with the court.

Pre-sentence investigators conduct lengthy background investigations and could recommend ADHD evaluation to the judge.

Probation officers have a great deal of contact with the offender and are probably best suited to ordering as a condition of probation an ADHD evaluation and follow-up treatment. Halfway house counselors share this strategic position.

Prison counselors and prison administrators, once educated on the impact of ADHD diagnosis and treatment, work in a setting that is ideal for coordinating evaluation, treatment, coaching on potential pitfalls upon discharge, and, most importantly, educating the prisoners about how ADHD affects their lives. Almost any prison guard or prison counselor will know many individuals in prison who seem pleasant and are doing well. They will tell their counselors that this is the last time they will be in prison and mean it. The counselors and other staff also believe this to be true. What we fail to see is prison is like real estate. Instead of location-location-location, for an ADHD inmate it is structure-structure structure. Their day is planned out for them, the day to day pressures of family, a job, bills, drug using friends and other distractions are not as prevelant. If the person has undiagnosed ADHD they will probably walk out of prison and be slapped in the face with all these day to day responsibilities and negative influences that were not present while in prison. It is easy to see how they can quickly revert back to their old life styles and find themselves right back in the criminal justice system. So education at the institutional level on ADHD and these other potential pitfalls should be addressed. Half-way house counselors and staff also see this scenario played out as a person is given more and more freedom of movement as they go through the program, only to seem to self sabatoge themselves at the very end or even abscond and take off. The pressures of life loom strongly and the glimmer of hope they had seen for themselves may start to fade as they realize they will struggle on the outside. We feel this is a major cause of recidivism in the criminal justice system.

Parole officers working with prison staff could implement the recommendation and act much as an ADHD coach does in trying to help the client stay on task, set goals, and mark achievement of those goals. The officer also acts as a sounding board for frustrations the individual may experience in readjusting to society.

SUMMARY AND CONCLUSION

Only when the criminal justice system is comprehensively knowledgeable about ADHD can we fully understand—by measuring, observing, and noting progress—the impact that this and perhaps other disorders have on the system. The effort comes with a relatively small price tag and is a worthwhile investment. With the cost of housing inmates also spinning out of control, the time to take action is now.

SPINNING OUT OF CONTROL

END NOTES

1 This estimate of the percentage of individuals in the criminal justice system that have ADHD is based upon studies in prison and studies of antisocial behavior in the community (Brown, 2003b; Chemers, 2002; Kapuchinski, 2000; Vermeiren, 2003; Vitelli, 1996; Washbusch, 2002). Note that the rate of ADHD in a normal population is about 9-12 percent (Farone, 2003).

2 "Fighting the Fog," by Tom Cradit, http://www.ldonline.org/first_person/cradit.html

3 Polis, B. (2003). "Only a mother could love him." ADDHelpGuide.

4 Robert Stalkup. Attention! Magazine, June 2003, p. 42.

5 Rubin, B. (1998). "Jack Sanders turns hyperactivity into measure of success." Chicago Tribune, November 6.

6 Case study cite by Lisa Belkin Office Messes, NY Times Magazine 7/18/04

7 Wolkenberg, F. (1987). "Out of darkness." New York Times, October 17.

8 The Conner's Adult ADHD Rating Scales (CAARS) is available online from the publisher, Multi-Health Systems, Inc. at www.mhs.com.

9 MTA refers to the National Institutes of Health Cooperative Multimodal Treatment Study of Children with ADHD. It included 579 elementary school children with ADHD, ages seven to nine, who were randomly assigned to four treatment conditions for 14 months: medication alone, psychosocial treatment alone, medication and psychosocial treatment combined, routine community care (Jensen et al., 2003; MTA Cooperative Group, 2004b).

RECOMMENDED READING

All About Attention Deficit Disorder
Thomas W. Phelan, Ph.D

Driven to Distraction: Recognizing and Coping with Attention Deficit Disorder from Childhood Through Adulthood
Edward Hallowell, MD & John Ratey, MD

Out of the Fog: Treatment Options and Coping Strategies for Adult Attention Deficit Disorder
Kevin R. Murphy, PhD

YOU MEAN I'M NOT LAZY, STUPID OR CRAZY?!: A Self-help Book for Adults with Attention Deficit Disorder
Kate Kelly & Peggy Ramundo

Attention-Deficit Hyperactivity Disorder in Adults
Paul H. Wender, MD

Adventures in Fast Forward: Life, Love, and Work for the Add Adult
Kathleen G. Nadeau

Answers to Distraction
Edward Hallowell, MD & John Ratey, MD

Attention Deficit Disorder in Adults
Lynn Weiss, Kenneth A. Bonnet PhD

Attention Deficit Disorder : A Different Perception
Thom Hartmann, Edward M. Hallowell, Michael Popkin

Women With Attention Deficit Disorder: Embracing
Disorganization at Home and in the Workplace
Sari Solden

Teenagers With ADD: A Parents' Guide
Chris A. Zeigler Dendy

Adult AD/HD: A Reader-Friendly Guide to Identifying,
Understanding, and Treating Adult Attention Deficit/Hyperactivity
Disorder
Michele Novotni, Thomas A. Whiteman

Journeys Through ADDulthood
Sari Solden

Taking Charge of ADHD, Revised Edition: The Complete,
Authoritative Guide for Parents
Russell A. Barkley

Healing ADD: The Breakthrough Program That Allows You
to See and Heal the 6 Types of ADD
Daniel G Amen, MD

1-2-3 Magic: Effective Discipline for Children 2-12
Thomas W. Phelan, Ph.D.

Surviving Your Adolescents: How to Manage and Let Go of
Your 13-18 Year Olds
Thomas W. Phelan, Ph.D.

Self-Esteem Revolutions in Children: Understanding & Managing the Critical Transitions in Your Child's Life
Thomas W. Phelan, Ph.D.

RECOMMENDED WEB SITES

http://addcorridorcoaching.com

http://www.chadd.org/

http://www.adders.org/

http://addwarehouse.com/shopsite_sc/store/html/index.html

http://add.about.com/library/weekly/?once=true&

http://my.webmd.com/content/article/66
/79556.htm?z=4199_000022207_TN_01

http://www.additudemag.com/

http://www.adddoctor.com/

http://vsa.vassar.edu/~source/drugs/antideps.html

http://www.healthyplace.com/Communities/ADD/Site/

http://www.help4adhd.org/

http://www.brainplace.com/bp/media/default.asp

http://www.addconsults.com/

http://www.drhallowell.com/

http://www.thrivewithadd.com/subscribe_popper

References

Ambroggio, J., & Jensen, P. (2002). Behavioral and medication treatments for ADHD – Comparisons and combinations. In Jensen, P., & Cooper, J. (2002). *Attention Deficit Hyperactivity Disorder,* (14:1-13). Civic Research Institute: Kingston, N.J.

American Academy of Pediatrics (2000). Clinical practice guideline: Diagnosis and evaluation of the child with attention-deficit/hyperactivity disorder. *Pediatrics, 105,* 1158-1168.

American Psychiatric Association. (2000). *Diagnostic and statistical manual of mental disorders* (Text rev.). Washington, DC: Author.

Arnold, E. (2002). Treatment alternatives for ADHD. In Jensen, P., & Cooper, J. (2002). *Attention Deficit Hyperactivity Disorder,* (13:1-13). Civic Research Institute: Kingston, N.J.

Arnold, L. E., Chuang, S., Davies, M., Abikoff, H. B., Conners, C. K., Elliott, G. R., et al. (2004). Nine months of multicomponent behavioral treatment for ADHD and effectiveness of MTA fading procedures. *Journal of Abnormal Child Psychology, 32,* 39-51.

Baddeley, A. (2001). Is working memory still working? *American Psychologist, November,* 851-855.

Barkley, R. (1997). Is ADHD an excuse for antisocial actions? *The ADHD Report, 5,* 1-2.

Barkley, R. (1998). *Attention-deficit hyperactivity disorder: A handbook for diagnosis and treatment.* (2nd ed.). New York: Guilford.

Barkley, R. (2002a). International consensus statement issued. *Clinical Child and Family Psychology Review, 5,* 89-111.

Barkley, R. (2002b). ADHD—Long-term course, adult outcome, and comorbid disorders. In P. Jensen & J. Cooper (Eds.), *Attention deficit hyperactivity disorder: State of the science – Best practices* (pp. 4:1-4:10). New Jersey: Civic Research Institute.

Barkley, R. (2003a). Editorial comment. *The ADHD Report, 11,* 7-8

Barkley, R. (2003b). Attention-deficit/hyperactivity disorder. In E. Mash & R. Barkley (Eds.), *Child Psychopathology* (2nd ed., pp. 75-143). New York: Guilford.

Barkley, R. (2004). Russ Barkley responds. *ADHD Report, 12,* 11-12.

Belkin, L. (2004) Office messes. *New York Times Magazine, July 18,* 24-29, 46, 54.

Bell, M. (2003). Dealing with the impact of AD/HD on marriage. *Attention!, April,* 19-23.

Biederman, J., Faraone, S., Mick, E., Williamson, S., Wilens, R., Spencer, T., Weber, W., Jetton, J., Kraus, I., Pert, J., Zallen, B. (1999). Clinical correlates of ADHD in females: findings from a large group of girls ascertained fro pediatric and psychiatric referral sources. *Journal of American Academy of Child & Adolescent Psychiatry, 38,* 966-976.

Brown, T. (1993). Attention deficit disorders without hyperactivity. *Chadder, Spring/Summer,* 7-10.

Brown, T. (2000). Emerging understandings of attention-deficit disorders and comorbidities. In T. Brown (Ed.), *Attention-deficit disorders and comorbidities in children, adolescents, and adults* (pp. 3-55). Washington: American Psychiatric Press, Inc.

Brown, T. (2003a, August). ADHD, age, and developmental demands on executive functions. In T. Brown (Chair), *ADHD and executive functions: Impact on age, gender, and new treatment options.* Symposium conducted at the meeting held in conjunction with the 111th Annual Convention of the American Psychological Association, August 7-10, Ontario, Canada.

Brown, T. (2003b). Personal communication. Symposium conducted at the meeting held in conjunction with the 111th Annual Convention of the American Psychological Association, August 7-10, Ontario, Canada.

Brown, T. (2004a). *Barriers to 'demystification of AD/HD and 'willpower'.* 10th Annual ADDA Conference, May 13-16, St Louis, Missouri.

Brown, T. (2004b). *Comorbidity in Adult AD/HD.* 10th Annual ADDA Conference, May 13-16, St Louis, Missouri.

Caspi, A., McClay, J., Moffitt, T.E., Mill, J., Martin, J., Craig, I.W., Taylor, A., & Poulton, R. (2002). Role of genotype in the cycle of violence in maltreated children. *Science, 297,* 851-854.

Castellanos, F. (2001). Neural substrates of ADHD. In D. Cohen, C. Goetz, & J. Jankovic (Eds.), *Tourette syndrome* (pp. 197-203). Philadelphia: Lippincott Williams & Wilkins.

Castellanos, F., Lee, P., Sharp, W., Jeffries, N., Greenstein, D., Clasen, L., Blumenthal, J., James, R., Ebens, C., Walter, J., Zijdenbos, A., Evans, A., Giedd, J., Rapoport, J. (2002). Developmental trajectories of brain volume abnormalities in children and adolescents with attention-deficit/hyperactivity disorder. *JAMA, 288,* 1740-1745.

Center for Science in the Public Interest (1999). Diet, ADHD & Behavior. *Quarter Century Review,* 1-34.

Chadd, 2000). AD/HD and the juvenile justice system. *Chadd Position Paper, 1-8.*

Chambers, R., Taylor, J., Potenza, M. (2003). Developmental neurocircuitry of motivation in adolescence: a critical period of addiction vulnerability. *American Journal of Psychiatry, 160,* 1041-1052.

Chemers, B. (2002). The impact of attention deficit hyperactivity disorder on the juvenile justice system. In P. Jensen & J. Cooper (Eds.), *Attention deficit hyperactivity disorder: State of the science – Best practices* (pp. 25:1-25:4). New Jersey: Civic Research Institute.

Christakis, D., Zimmerman, F., DiGiuseppe, D., & McCarty, C. (2004). Early television exposure and subsequent attentional problems in children. *Pediatrics, 113,* 708-713.

Collett, B., Ohan, J., & Myers, K. (2003). Ten-year review of rating scales. V: Scales assessing attention-deficit/hyperactivity disorder. *Journal of American Academy of Child & Adolescent Psychiatry, 42,* 1015-1037.

Connors, K. (2000). Attention-deficit/hyperactivity disorder--historical development and overview. *Journal of Attention Disorders, 3,* 173-190.

Courvoisie, H., Hooper, S., Fine, C., Kwock, L., & Castillo, M. (2004). *Journal of Neuropsychiatry and Clinical Neurosciences, 16,* 63-69.

Dendy, C. (2002). Five components of executive performance and how they impact school performance. *Attention!, February,* 26-30.

Doyle, A., Biederman, J., Seidman, L., Weber, W., Faraone, S. (2000). Diagnostic efficiency of neuropsychological test scores for discriminating boys with and without attention deficit-hyperactivity disorder. *Journal of Consulting and Clinical Psychology, 68,* 477-488.

Doyle, R. (2003, May). Reducing crime: Rehabilitation is making a comeback. *Scientific American*, May, 33A.

Ernst, M., Kimes, A., London, E., Matochik, J., Eldreth, D., Tata, S., Contoreggi, C., Leff, M., Bolla, K. (2003). Neural substrates of decision making in adults with attention deficit hyperactivity disorder. *American Journal of Psychiatry, 160*, 1061-1070.

Farone, S. (2003). *ADHD: Fact and fiction*. Symposium conducted at the meeting held in conjunction with the 111th Annual Convention of the American Psychological Association, August 7-10, Ontario, Canada.

Fischer, M., & Barkley, R. (2003). Childhood ADHD and later antisocial behavior and drug use. *The ADHD Report, 11*, 6-11.

Frick, P., & Morris, A. (2004). Temperament and developmental pathways to conduct problems. *Journal of Clinical Child and Adolescent Psychology, 33*, 54-68.

Fisher, S., Francks, C., McCracken, J., McGough, J., Marlow, A., MacPhie, L., Newbury, D., Crawford, L., Palmer, C., Woodward, J., Del'Homme, M., Cantwell, D., Nelson, S., Monaco, A., & Smalley, S. (2002). A genomewide search for loci involved in attention-deficit/hyperactivity disorder. *American Journal of Human Genetics, 70,* 1183-1196.

Goldman, L, & Bezman, R. (1998). Diagnosis and treatment of attention deficit/hyperactivity disorder. *Journal of the American Medical Association, 279,* 1100-1107.

Goldstein, S. (1997). Attention-deficit/hyperactivity disorder: Implications for the criminal justice system. *FBI Publications: Law Enforcement Bulletin, June,* 1-10.

Goldstein, S. (2003). Symptoms vs. impairment: The role of impairment in diagnosing AD/HD. *Attention!, June,* 21-29.

Goldstein, S., Gordon, M. (2003). Gender issues and ADHD: Sorting fact from fiction. *The ADHD Report, August,* 7-16.

Gomez, R., Burns, G., Walsh, J., Alves de Moura, M., (2003). A multitrait-multisource confirmatory factor analytic approach to the construct validity of ADHD rating scales. *Psychological Assessment, 15.* 3-16.

Gordon, M., & Barkley, R. (1998). Tests and observational measures. In R. Barkley (Ed.), *Attention-deficit hyperactivity disorder* (pp.294). New York: Guilford Press.

Gordon, M., Goldstein, S., Barkley, R., Murphy, K. (2003) Letters. *Monitor on Psychology, April*, 10.

Grodzinsky, Ga., & Barkley, R. (1999). Predictive power of frontal lobe tests in the diagnosis of attention deficit hyperactivity disorder. *The Clinical Neuropsychologist, 13*, 12-21.

Hallowell, E. (1993). Living and loving with attention deficit disorder: couples where one partner has ADD. *Chadder, Spring/Summer*, 13-18.

Hinshaw, S. P. (2003). A family perspective on mental disorder: Silence, stigma, diagnosis, treatment, and resilience. *The ADHD Report, 11*, 1-6.

Hinshaw, S., Carte, E., Sami N., Treuting, J., Zupan, B. (2002). Preadolescent girls with attention-deficit/hyperactivity disorder: II. Neuropsychological performance in relation to subtypes and individual classification. *Journal of Consulting and Clinical Psychology, 70*, 1099-1111.

Hinshaw, S., & Lee, S. (2003). Conduct and oppositional defiant disorders. In E. Mash & R. Barkley (Eds.), *Child psychopathology* (pp. 14-198). New York: Guilford.

Imperio, W., & Anderson, L. (2004). Annual conference recapitulation. *Attention, February,* 25-34.

Jensen, P. S., Abikoff, H. B., Arnold, L. E., Epstein, J., Greenhill, L. L., Hechtman, L., et al. (2003). A 24-month follow-up to the NIMH MTA study. *Attention!, December,* 22-25.

Kapuchinski, S. (2000). Examining AD/HD's role in incarceration. *Attention!, July/August,* 50-53.

Klein, R., Abikoff, H., Klass, E., Ganeles, D., Seese, L., & Pollack, S. (1997). Clinical efficacy of methylphenidate in conduct disorder with and without attention deficit hyperactivity disorder. *Archives of General Psychiatry, 54,* 1073-1080.

Klein-Schwartz, W., & McGrath, J. (2003). Poison centers' experience with methylphenidate abuse in pre-teens and adolescents. *Journal of the American Academy of Child and Adolescent Psychiatry, 42,* 288-294.

Kohlberg, J. (2002). AD/HD and organization: A collision course? *Attention!, October,* 17-20.

Lahey, B., McBurnett, K., & Loeber, R. (2000). In A. Sameroff, M. Lewis, & S. Millers (Eds.), *Handbook of Developmental Psychopathology* (2nd ed., pp. 431-446). New York: Kluwer Academic/Plenum Publishers.

Loo, S. (2003). EEG and neurofeedback findings in ADHD. *The ADHD Report, 11,* 1-6.

Loo, S. (2004). The EEG and ADHD: Reply to Monastra. *ADHD Report, 12, 9-10.*

Lykken, D. (2001). Parental licensure. *American Psychologist, November,* 885-894.

Lynam, D. (1996). Early identification of chronic offenders: Who is the fledgling psychopath? *Psychological Bulletin, 120,* 209-234.

MacDonald, A. (2003). Imaging studies bring ADHD into sharper focus. *Brain Work, 13,* 1-2.

Mackintosh, N. & Bennett, E. (2003). The fractionation of working memory maps onto different components of intelligence *Intelligence, 31,* 519-531.

McCabe, K., Rodgers, C., Yeh, M., & Bough, R. (2004). Gender differences in childhood onset conduct disorder. *Development and Psychopathology, 16,* 179-192.

McGuffin, P., Riley, B., & Plomin, R. (2001). Toward behavioral genomics. *Science, 291,* 1248-49.

Milch, R., Balentine, A., & Lynam, D. (2001). The predominantly inattentive subtype-not a subtype. *ADHD Report, 10,* 1-6.

Miller, D. & Blum, K. (1996). *Overload – Attention deficit disorder and the addictive brain.* Kansas City, KS: Andrews and McMeel.

Mirsky, A., & Duncan, C. (2003).The attention battery for children: A systematic approach. In G. Goldstein, S. Beers, & M. Herson, (Eds.), *Comprehensive handbook of psychological assessment.* New York: Wiley.

Monastra, V. (2004). EEG and neurofeedback findings in ADHD: An empirical Response. *ADHD Report, 12,* 5-8.

MTA Cooperative Study (2004a). National Institute of Health mental health multimodal treatment study of ADHD follow-up: 24-month outcomes of treatment strategies for Attention Deficit/Hyperactivity Disorder. *Pediatrics, 113,* 754-761.

MTA Cooperative Study (2004b). National Institute of
     Health mental health multimodal treatment study of
     ADHD follow-up: Changes in effectiveness and
     growth after end of treatment. *Pediatrics, 113,* 762-769.

Murphy, K. (1995). *Out of the fog.* New York: Hyperion.

Nadeau, K. (2000). Elementary school girls with AD/HD.
     Attention!, July/Aug., 44-49.

Nadeau, K. (2003). Letters. *Monitor on Psychology, April,* 10.

Nadeau, K., Littman, E., Quinn, P. (1999). *Understanding girls
     with attention deficit hyperactivity disorder.* Silver Spring,
     MD: Advantage Books.

The National Resource Center On ADHD (2004).
     Medication management for adults with ADHD.
     Information & Resources Sheet #11.

Newcorn, J. (2003, August). Evaluating new medication
     options for the treatment of ADHD. In T. Brown
     (Chair), *ADHD and executive functions: Impact on age,
     gender, and new treatment options._*Symposium conducted
     at the meeting held in conjunction with the 111th
     Annual Convention of the American Psychological
     Association, Ontario, Canada.

Nigg, J. (2001). Is ADHD a disinhibitory disorder? *Psychological Bulletin, 127,* 571-598.

Nigg, J. (2003). ADHD: Guides for the perplexed reflect the state of the field. *Journal of Clinical Child and Adolescent Psychology, 32,* 302-308.

Olfson, M., Gameroff, M. J., Marcus, S. C., & Jensen, P. S. (2003). National trends in the treatment of attention deficit hyperactivity disorder. *American Journal of Psychiatry, 160,* 1071-1077.

Pfiffner, L. (2003). Psychosocial treatment for ADHD-Inattentive type. *The ADHD Report, 11,* 1-3.

Pinker, S. (2002). *The blank slate.* New York: Penguin.

Pliszka, S. (2002). Neuroimaging and ADHD: Recent progress. *The ADHD Report, 10,* 1-6.

Polis, B. (2003). *Only a mother could love him.* ADDHelpGuide.

Quinn, P., & Nadeau, K. (Eds.). (2002). *Gender issues and AD/HD: Research, diagnosis, and treatment.* Silver Springs, MD: Advantage Books.

Rabiner, D., Palsson, O., & Freer, P. (2003). Does neurofeedback help kids with AD/HD? *Attention, December,* 31-34.

Reiff, M., & Tippins, S. (2004). *ADHD: A complete and authoritative guide.* American Academy of Pediatrics.

Robin, A. (2001). Can your marriage survive ADHD? *Attention!, June,* 7-12.

Rowland, A., Lesesne, C., & Abramowitz, A. (2002). The Epidemiology of attention-deficit/hyperactivity disorder (ADHD): A public health view. *Mental Retardation and Developmental Disabilities Research Reviews, 8,* 162-170.

Rutter, M. (2003). Commentary: Nature-nurture interplay in emotional disorders. *Journal of Child Psychology and Psychiatry, 44,* 934-944.

Rutter, M. & Silberg, J. (2002). Gene-environment interplay in relation to emotional and behavioral disturbance. *Annual Reviews Psychology, 53,* 463-490.

Sandberg, S. (Ed.). (2002). *Hyperactivity and attention disorders of childhood* (2nd ed.). Cambridge, England: Cambridge University Press.

Sonuga-Barke, E. (2002). Psychological heterogeneity in AD/HD-A dual pathway model of behavior and cognition. *Behavioral Brain Research, 130,* 29-36.

Tannock, R. (2003, August). Girls with ADHD: Cognitive and psychosocial impairments. In T. Brown (Chair), *ADHD and executive functions: Impact on age, gender, and new treatment options.*_Symposium conducted at the meeting held in conjunction with the 111th Annual Convention of the American Psychological Association, Ontario, Canada.

Todd, R., Rasmussen, E., Wood, C., Levy, F., & Hay, D. (2004). Should sluggish cognitive tempo be included in the diagnosis of Attention-Deficit/Hyperactivity Disorder? *Journal of the American Academy of Child and Adolescent Psychiatry, 43,* 588-597.

Tully, L., Arseneault, L., Caspi, A., Moffitt, T., & Morgan, J. (2004). Does maternal warmth moderate the effects of birth weight on twins' Attention-Deficit/Hyperactivity Disorder (ADHD) symptoms and low IQ? *Journal of Consulting and Clinical Psychology, 72,* 218-226.

Tuma, R. (2004). Why only some become addicted. *Brain Work, January-February,* 1, 10.

Vermeiren, R. (2003). Psychopathology and delinquency in adolescents: A descriptive and developmental perspective. *Clinical Psychology Review, 23*, 277-318.

Vitelli, R. (1996). Prevalence of childhood conduct and attention-deficit hyperactivity disorders in adult maximum-security inmates. *International Journal of Offender Therapy and Comparative Criminology, 40*, 263-271.

Waschbusch, D. (2002). A meta-analytic examination of comorbid hyperactive-impulsive- attention problems and conduct problems. *Psychological Bulletin, 128*, 118-150.

Wasserman, G., Jensen, P., Ko, S., Cocozza, J., Trupin, E., Angold, A., Cauffman, E., & Grisso, T. (2003). Mental health assessments in juvenile justice: Report on the consensus conference. *Journal of American Academy of Child & Adolescent Psychiatry, 42*, 752-761.

Watson, J. (2003). DNA: *The secret of life*. New York: Knopf Publishing

Weiss. M., Hechtaman, L., & Weiss, G. (2000). ADHD in parents. *Journal of the American Academy of Child and Adolescent Psychiatry, 39*, 1059-1061.

Wender, P. (1995). *Attention-deficit hyperactivity disorder in adults.*
New York, NY: Oxford University Press.

Wilens, T. (2003). *Does the pharmacotherapy of ADHD beget later substance abuse?* A meta-analytic review of the literature. Symposium conducted at the meeting held in conjunction with the 111th Annual Convention of the American Psychological Association, Ontario, Canada.

Wilens, T. E., Faraone, S. V., Biederman, J., & Gunawardene, S. (2003). Does stimulant therapy of attention-deficit/hyperactivity disorder beget later substance abuse? A meta-analytic review of the literature. *Pediatrics, 111,* 179-185.

Wilens, T. E., Spencer, T. J., & Biederman, J. (2000). Attention-deficit/hyperactivity disorder with substance use disorders. In T. E. Brown (Ed.). *Attention-deficit disorders and comorbidities in children, adolescents, and adults* (pp. 319-339). Washington, DC: American Psychiatric Press, Inc.

Willoughby, M. (2003). Developmental course of ADHD symtomatology during the transition from childhood to adolescence: a review with recommendations. *Journal of Child Psychology and Psychiatry, 44,* 88-106.

Zametkin, A. (2002). ADHD: Smoking and stimulants. *The ADHD Report, December,* 4-6.

INDEX

A

Abnormalities, 34, 51, 57
Abuse, 44, 55
Academic Difficulties, 15, 16, 17, 18, 19, 20, 80, 87, 98, 115
Acceptance By Others, 66, 67, 91, 92
Accidental Injuries-Non Motor Vehicle, 54, 88, 98
Accountability, 117
Accurate Screening Needed, 85, 87, 92, 95, 96, 97, 98, 99, 104, 125
Acquired Brain Damage, 54
Act Guilty, 9, 63, 64, 65, 68
Acting On Dares, 88,
Activity, 8, 15, 29, 48, 51, 55, 60, 64, 65, 66
Acupuncture - As an Alternative Treatment?, 114
Adderall, 109
Adderall XR, 109
Addictive Drugs, 45, 47,
ADHD-

> *A Real Developmental Brain Disorder (Consensus)*, 2, 49
> *Adoption – Increased Risk For Having It*, 51
> *Adults*, 20, 27, 36, 45, 100, 107, 110, 111, 112
> *Appearance Of Indifference To Pending Charges*, 73
> *Areas That May Mimic It*, 55, 57
> *Attitude Toward "The System" Poor*, 22, 122
> *Blaming Oneself*, 86
> *Brain Disorder*, 2, 49
> *Causes*, 3, 49, 54, 56
> *Client Can Be Defense Attorneys Worst Nightmare*, 77
> *Client Often Familiar To Police, Prosecutors & Judge*, 7, 10, 60, 62, 65, 67, 76,86, 102
> *Coaches*, 105, 116, 117, 118, 126, 127

Anti Social Behavior, 5, 7, 10, 16, 28, 30, 31, 40, 41, 42, 43, 44, 45, 48

Apologetic, 10

Appearances-Overall, 9, 17, 24, 25, 37, 38, 39, 64, 65, 80, 97, 101

Appear Suspicious, 9, 64

Appetite Reduction, 112

Appointments, 20, 21, 24, 25, 74, 75, 77, 78, 89, 117, 122

Appropriate Treatment, 36, 96, 97, 116

Argumentative / Defiant, 10, 43, 55, 116, 121

Arithmetic Pills, 106

Arraignments, 74

Arrest, Introduction, 7, 9, 24, 64, 71, 72, 74, 85, 88

Asking A Lot Of Questions, 9, 61, 81, 87, 91, 119

Assaults, 80, 88

Assignments - Not Completed, 20, 26, 32, 108

Attempting Suicide, 31, 33, 35, 71

Attention, 1, 2, 4, 5, 7, 11, 12, 13, 14, 15, 16, 19, 20, 21, 22, 23, 24, 25, 26, 27, 29, 46, 47, 48, 50, 52, 53, 54, 55, 57, 59, 64, 68, 72, 73, 91, 106, 108, 125

Attitude, 22, 36, 37, 63, 122

Attorney / Lawyer, Introduction, 24, 25, 68, 69, 71, 74, 75, 76, 77, 78, 79, 82, 117, 126

Authority Figures, 10, 16, 18, 29, 59, 62, 63, 68, 80, 86, 92, 102

Autism, 50

Avoid Quiet Activities, 8

B

Background Investigation, 72, 79, 80, 126

Bed Never Made, 34

Behavior Problems, Introduction, 1, 2, 3, 4, 5, 6, 7, 8, 9, 10, 16, 17, 28, 29, 30, 31, 34, 37, 40, 41, 42, 43, 44, 45, 48, 50, 51, 52, 53, 59, 60, 61, 62, 63, 64, 66, 72, 75, 77, 87, 88, 96, 98, 103, 106, 115, 125

F

G

Isolation, 18, 26, 91

N

O

P

S

X,Y,Z